Acclaim for

Standing in Your Power; A Gu

"This thoughtfully written book will be joyfully devoured by any woman seeking validation, empowerment and tools to grow forward."

— Stephanie Staples author of *When Enlightening Strikes – Creating a Mindset for Uncommon Success*

"I love the way Debbie intersperses words of wisdom with stories that captured my attention in an empathetic embrace and bring life to the concepts she shares. With gentle and loving guidance, Debbie helps the reader peel back the mind's layers to reveal beliefs that shape one's life, and then offers practical steps to apply the concepts in one's own life."

— Maggie Reigh, author of *9 Ways to Bring Out the Best in You & Your Child*

"*Standing in Your Power* not only reveals sound principles and tools which can quickly move you along your path of personal growth, but also introduces you to a wonderful, relatable character named Jane who represents our very human struggle with being our best selves. Consider this book your manual for discovering the power you already have within you!"

— Deb Dawson-Dunn, Life Coach, Speaker and owner of Get It Dunn

"*Standing in Your Power* is a wonderful book full of wisdom, entertaining stories, practical tips and exercises for discovering your potential as a human being and living a happy and confident life. Whether you are looking for radical improvement in your life, or just continuous personal development, I highly recommend this book to guide you through finding your personal power to live your best life."

— Shawnda Muir, author of *Cancer Scores a Hat Trick; Lessons About Living Life to the Fullest*

"Debbie Pokornik uses her outstanding skills of persuasion to present a straight-forward and engaging read. She helps us to 'wake up', embrace change, and live an empowered life. We can all relate to the character, Jane's, journey; and through learning about her, we find out how to 'take a stand' and propel our own personal development pathway. I recommend this book to anyone looking for a relatable reference for living their best life."

— Deri Latimer, inspirational speaker and author of *Wake Up to Your Habits*

"Debbie teaches you how to tap into your feminine wisdom and be more alert to your emotional energy. This book offers a wealth of insights on how to change what isn't working in your life, be holistically assertive and personally empowered."

— Jacquie Nagy, Owner of Holistic Directions Inc., NLP Trainer and Performance Coach

"*Standing in Your Power* is like a 'toolbox' to getting what you want in life and discovering your inner strength and beauty in the process. Use this book to help you release negative energy and let "Jane" guide you to embrace your life's journey!"

— Diane Drawbridge, School Principal

"I know from personal experience and from my coaching and consulting work with women business owners just how hard it is for women to truly claim their own power. Exploring limiting beliefs like aggression vs. assertion, and learning how to tune in to your own body and guidance system is invaluable and life changing. Debbie, and the story of Jane, do a wonderful job of "gently shoving" the reader toward a new source of power - the one each one of us already has."

— Sherri Garrity, consultant and equine guided learning coach

"*Standing in Your Power* is thoroughly engaging on many levels. First of all, Debbie Pokornik is a wonderful writer, so while you're gently tugged through your own a-ha's and the author's many insights about your personal life journey, you will absolutely delight in the ride. Secondly, this is a book you'll actually use. You'll want to have a good supply of highlighters and a place to take notes as you read. Pokornik's book is so chock-full of sound advice, thought-provoking wisdom, and practical solutions, you'll feel compelled to record details and your own reminders – I foresee my own copy as soon-to-be dog-eared and filled with sticky notes. I'll use this book with my own business coaching clients, who sometimes make their own journeys 'harder and less enjoyable,' for sure."

— Marcia Hoeck, helping values-based entrepreneurs reach their goals faster with A Purposeful Business.com

"*Standing in Your Power* is a well-written book, filled with hope and optimism. As I was reading, I felt like I was interacting with a trusted, supportive friend. I enjoyed the strategies for enhancing confidence, acceptance, and self-awareness and have already begun to implement some of the goddess tips. As a result of reading this book I feel energized and less nervous about making changes in my life."

— Catherine Tsagarakis, PhD, C. Psych.

"The hardest thing for me to do is ask for help whether personally or professionally. Realizing it is not a sign of weakness was a real eye-opener for me . . . we all need help and support from others at different points in our lives and that's ok. Debbie's ability to show woman they are strong, smart, perfect in their own right and have the capacity to stand in their power will inspire all who read this book."

— Rhonda Taylor, working mom and Regional Manager for Frontier College

"We, society as a whole, are on the cusp of much needed positive change. Think of this book as the catalyst for working in that direction! We are women; hear us roar; you know, as we raise the bar for ourselves and for the next generation. Learn and grow while laughing and crying, it really is the best way. This book is for everyone who wants the best for themselves, and who doesn't want the best?"

— Frances Cooper, mom, artist, engineering aide

"If you are so busy "doing" that you forget to feel the joy, love and fulfillment of a life well lived, then this book is for you. *Standing in Your Power* will teach you simple ways to connect to your core and provide a reminder that you, being you, is exactly right."

— Dr. Lori Petrilli, chiropractor

"Debbie Pokornik's book provides ideas that are thought provoking and soul searching. Her stories of real life situations are very relevant. Through gentle persuasion, she provides tools so you can examine your own journey and look inward to "Live Your Life Fully Awake.""

— Helen Dyrkacz, professional speaker, trainer, and facilitator

"Do you sense that something is missing in your life but you're not sure what? Then you must read *Standing In Your Power*. You will not only learn how to tap into your Inner Wisdom but discover what you are really here on this Earth for."

— Trisha Sveistrup, www.TrishaSveistrup.com

Reading *Standing in Your Power* is like having a cup of tea and a chat with a good friend. Debbie writes in an everyday conversational style, but gets right to the heart of what many woman are feeling. Following 'Jane' we are able to relate to her troubles which allow us to take a step back and look at our own life objectively. Doing so, and with Debbie's guidance we start to accept new possibilities.

— Noreen Kolesar, Owner of Mindstage

Standing in Your Power

A Guide for Living Your Life Fully Awake

Debbie Pokornik, BA, BSW

Standing in Your Power, A Guide for Living Your Life Fully Awake
Copyright © November 2012 by Debbie Pokornik, BA, BSW

All rights reserved. No part of this book may be used or reproduced by any means, graphic, electronic or mechanical, including photocopying, recording, taping or by any information storage retrieval system without the written permission of the publisher except in the case of brief quotations embodied in critical articles and reviews.

Empowering NRG may be contacted via the following:

www.empoweringnrg.com

mail@empoweringnrg.com

Box 23, Grp 70, R.R. #1
Anola, Manitoba, Canada
R0E 0A0

Because of the dynamic nature of the Internet, any Web addresses or links contained in this book may have changed since publication and may no longer be valid.

Cover photo: Bigstock.com/Gino Santa Maria

Book layout and cover design: Teresa Dawn, Imagine Graphic Design
www.imagineu.ca

Deanna,

Our journeys are unique — it's up to us to make them special. I'm so glad we connected!

Other Books by Debbie Pokornik

Break Free of Parenting Pressures
Embrace Your Natural Guidance

I Don't Want to Punish My Child, But What Else can I do?
5 Things Every Parent Must Know About Discipline

I Love You, But at This Moment I Don't Like You Very Much . . .
Understanding and Strengthening the Parent-Child Relationship

*To the women in my life who have helped me
explore personal power in so many ways.*

*You are beautiful souls and
I thank you for joining me on this journey.*

Contents

Preface i

Introduction v

A Powerful You 1
1: You are Incomparable 1
2: You are Perfect Just as You Are 7
You Are Perfect – Now Let's Fix You! 9

Common Power Drains 11
3: How to Quiet the Voice that Keeps Putting You Down 11
4: The BIG 5 Patterns of Self-Destruction 17
Why Boundaries Help Us Feel Whole 21

A Challenge to the Feminine 24
5: Honoring the Feminine in a Masculine World 25
6: Reconnecting With Your Feminine Side 33
How the Divine Feminine Can Help Us 40

Believing it into Existence 42
7: What Do You Believe? 42
8: Limiting Beliefs 47

When Power is a Problem 52
9: Standing Up For Yourself Assertively 52
10: When Assertion Becomes Aggression 56
Standing Up for You – How it's Done 60

Increasing Awareness 63
11: Practicing Self-Control 63
12: Creating I-messages 71
How Expectations Become Irreconcilable Differences 77

Your Inner Wisdom 82
13: Sharing Your Expectations Clearly 82
14: Choosing Inner Wisdom 88
Ego, Meet Your New Boss 93

Where Do You Focus Your Energy? 95
15: Tomorrow's a Flirt, But Today is a Keeper 95
16: Fill'er Up! How Self-Care Can Keep You Going 101
Having a Sweet Body 107

Putting It All Together 109
17: Loving Your Life 109
18: Releasing the Pressure 113
A Life of Learning 122

Conclusion 128
Embracing Your Journey 128
Jane's Epilogue 131
Acknowledgments 133
Suggested Resources 135

Jane's Story

Meet Jane xi
.... 4
.... 8
.... 14
.... 19
.... 31
.... 39
.... 44
.... 49
.... 51
.... 57
.... 62
.... 68
.... 74
.... 80
.... 86
.... 91
.... 97
.... 104
.... 111
.... 119
.... 125
Jane's Epilogue 129

Preface

I started my first serious career job when my dad talked to a friend high up in a Canadian bank and landed me an interview. I was so nervous at the interview I could barely type (I think my best test was 25 words per minute). I wasn't sure what typing had to do with working at a bank, but I decided that if typing was important, I had just ruined my only chance.

Imagine my excitement when a week later I was hired as a stenographer and would start training the following Monday. I was so proud of myself, even though I didn't know what a stenographer was, and couldn't wait for my dad to get home, so I could tell him.

A month before turning eighteen, I walked into a large downtown branch to be trained as a stenographer, which turned out to be a fancy name for secretary. There were two stenos at this branch who took turns showing me the ropes.

Less than two weeks later, a job opened up at a smaller branch with only one steno and I was told to report there on Monday morning. I was terrified!

The girl I was replacing was "leaving the bank forever"; in other words, she didn't really care what kind of mess she left the place in. She told me which clients to avoid, which ones would talk my ear off and which ones I should jump up to serve immediately. I took the details all in, wondering how I was going to do everything once she disappeared a few days later. "Just do the must-get-done things first," she said. "You'll be fine."

At the end of the week, she left behind a mound of to be filed items, an inbox full of typing that was needed yesterday and a very shaky steno looking much like a deer caught in the headlights. I did as she said, focused on the absolute musts, and slowly got into a routine.

Shortly after I started working there a new branch administration officer was put in place as my boss. She was also quite young, fresh out of university, and determined to excel in the banking world. She didn't smile often – at least not in my direction.

Despite this situation, I was feeling pretty comfortable with the routine I had created by the time my three month appraisal came up for review. Imagine my surprise when I was told that I was not meeting expectations; in fact, it was only because of my dad's connection that she was extending my probation rather than firing me!

I couldn't believe it. My bosses had always loved my work. I wanted the ground to open up and swallow me whole, but that didn't happen. You see, I rode to work with my dad every day and when I left work there he was, waiting for me. With tears flowing, I told him what had happened.

"Obviously," he said, "she hasn't seen the real you yet. Guess you're just going to have to show her how you can shine." Those were his only words.

At first I wanted to tell him that I was quitting, my boss was right and I wasn't cut out for that job. But the words stuck in my throat. Unable to speak, I reflected on what he'd said and realized he was right.

I wasn't shining at work. I was just getting the 'must-do' pieces done. In fact, I had gotten so deep into self-doubt, uncertainty, worry, fear and guilt that the real me wasn't shining through at all.

I developed a plan to break free of these shackles that I had put upon myself - take back my personal power, stand on my own and show my boss how capable I was. I became a star employee and started training new staff the day I finished my extended probation.

That was the first time I consciously recognized that I was not standing in my power. It was also the first inkling of a realization that only I could change my situation.

After several years of continual growth with the bank, I felt a 'gentle shove' from the universe to make a change. I decided to apply to university thinking I would like to work with the deaf and hearing impaired.

At the time, my decision felt quite random and scary. Many people questioned my judgment and wondered why I would leave a promising career to go back to school when I had been a less than 'C' average student.

Subsequently, I excelled at University finishing a Bachelor of Arts Degree in two years and a Bachelor of Social Work three years later. I had an excellent grade point average and proved that a voluntary student is much more capable than a resistant one.

During this time, I also met my husband, got married, had my first child (a second one followed a couple years later), bought a house and moved more than an hour away from my main support system.

After graduation, I learned more life lessons. I struggled to find a job, dealt with a major health issue, lost my home in a flood and was let-go from a job. I also started a business that never moved beyond the 'expensive hobby' phase and was involved in a traumatic accident that upset my sense of balance for nearly a year.

I share this with you, not for pity or applause, but so you are aware that my life has not been easy. I've grown enormously from each of my lessons - physically, mentally, emotionally, socially and spiritually. I've maintained my positive outlook on life and have enjoyed the journey - bumps and all.

From the context of my life experience, including formal education, divine inspiration and spiritual enlightenment, I have developed the contents of this book.

I hope you enjoy the book and feel the love, understanding and acceptance intended on every page.

Introduction

Have you ever experienced a situation where you felt fantastic, or even on top of the world? At that moment, you know you can handle whatever life throws your way, no matter how hard it is. This situation provides a wonderful feeling of strength, confidence and worthiness.

If you're like most people, it's likely you've also experienced the opposite. Moments when you feel uncertain whether you have what it takes to do whatever you've set out to do. Self-doubt, worry and fear of making a total mess of things lies right around the corner, making you wonder why you ever thought you could handle the task in the first place. This experience makes you feel weak, incapable and unworthy.

If you've ever felt this way and especially if it occurs on a regular basis, then this book is for you. It is time for you to stand in your power - to recognize the unique and wonderful individual you are and become aware of all the things you are accidentally doing to hold yourself back. You are not destined to struggle throughout life and this book will help you understand how to overcome your obstacles.

On the other hand, maybe you are a person who has experienced a disempowering moment on occasion, but overall, you appear to have it all together. People see you as confident, capable and clearly moving along your path in a positive direction. Yet you know this is not always the case and at times feel discontent.

This situation probably makes you feel quite guilty or even greedy because it appears you've got it all and yet you want something more, or at least something different.

Let me assure you that this is not greed or anything to feel guilty about. It's actually harder to sell the need for an upgrade than to justify fixing things when they are obviously broken. Most of us have been taught the old adage, "If it ain't broke, don't fix it," and have internalized this message, as if to do anything else would be wrong.

I disagree. Feeling that pull to do something more, that desire to shake things up when all is going well is what I refer to as a 'gentle shove' from the universe. There is something more you feel drawn to do and the universe is suggesting you get to it. My experience with universal suggestions is that if you don't pay attention to the gentle shove, the next suggestion will feel more like a whack.

Personal growth is something we do continuously throughout life. In fact, it is life! At this time in our world, hundreds of thousands of women are feeling the pull to make significant changes in their lives. You are not alone in this situation, and this compelling feeling you are experiencing is not a coincidence.

Consequently, if you are a confident, capable and successful person who feels a yearning to do something more, congratulations for recognizing this need; be assured this book is for you as well.

About the Book

Standing In Your Power is geared at empowering people, especially women, to let go of the negative energies that are holding them back and reconnect to their inner wisdom and strength. The book demystifies what personal power is all about in easy-to-read chapters on boundaries, relationships, inner critics, limiting beliefs and being assertive.

The book shares important information on the Divine Feminine - how to embrace this feminine energy and why our society can no longer afford to overlook the need to rebalance in this area. It includes **Taking a Stand** sections with ideas for putting what you are learning into action as well as **Oh My Goddess!** hints which offer quick, easily implemented, tips to guide you towards immediate and positive results. While this book was written with women in mind, the information is universal and relevant to anyone who is open to reading it.

Throughout the pages, you're also going to meet a woman named Jane. She is loosely based on people I've worked with over the years; her story helps to make the information real as well as more entertaining.

So, if you're ready to make permanent, positive changes in your life, turn the page and let's get started.

Embracing Change

If you're like me, you likely feel a blend of nervousness, excitement and uncertainty when anyone suggests making changes in your life. The truth is that intentionally doing things differently is a challenging task. To make it easier for you and to help you get the most out of this book, I'd like to introduce some common responses to change and what you can do to use them to your advantage.

Resonance – The new idea feels good to you and resonates beautifully, much like when two voices harmonize perfectly. It feels right, perhaps like a missing piece has been found and you cannot wait to give it a try. You embrace the change and are shocked when others don't seem quite so enthusiastic.

When a new idea resonates with you, it's time to celebrate and enjoy the new-found treasure.

Regular – This plain word perfectly describes the feeling people have about a lot of new ideas. Nothing feels different - you don't feel excited or repulsed - you just feel regular. It's important to know about this category, because this one causes many people to 'should' on themselves.

Since the idea makes sense and you don't feel strongly for or against it, you add it on your 'to do' list and then feel guilty when you don't put it into practice, or stressed because of all the things on your list.

Beware of new ideas that make you think "I **should** do that" without strong feelings one way or the other. Just because you can, doesn't mean you should.

Resistance - In this case, the new idea feels wrong, repulsive or uncomfortable. This is, by far, the most common reaction to change, yet also the least understood. Feeling resistant to change can indicate a variety of things and our response will be different, depending on the meaning.

To make it easier for you to deal with resistance to ideas in this book, here are three things to keep in mind:

i) **Comfort Zone Alert!** The most common reason for resistance to a new idea comes from fear of moving out of your comfort zone. The suggested change is going to cause you to grow and there is always a risk with growing. In an attempt to protect you from 'upsetting the apple cart,' your ego creates resistance, making you feel as if growing right now would be a bad idea.

You can recognize this type of resistance because you will find yourself justifying nonconformity or looking for all the reasons that this idea will not work. You'll quickly become defensive, which is a common emotional response to fear, and may find yourself wanting to attack the idea itself.

Remedy: Know that you are perfectly safe and capable of moving to the next level. Take the change one step at a time and know that you are deserving of it then get ready to move forward.

ii) **Personal Block.** Another possibility for resistance to change is that you have a personal block getting in the way of the idea taking shape. Typically, this block is connected to a memory or belief that makes you think you are unworthy of something. This resistance offers you a chance to release the block or heal the negative energies from your previous experience.

You will recognize this form of resistance because it will typically result in a desire to run away rather than confront the issue. It is often fear-based, but tends to result in a wish to avoid rather than attack.

Remedy: It's time to deal with this block. As long as you ignore it, you will feel stuck in the same place. Opportunity will continue to present itself, but unless you take steps to remove the block, you will become frustrated and down-hearted. Find a coach, therapist or shaman. Take a program or read books on releasing limiting beliefs. Find what works for you and do it.

iii) **Intuition.** Last but not least, resistance could indicate an instinctual knowledge that this idea is not good for you. In this case, the resistance is your intuition warning you that this change would be a detour from your path and is unnecessary for you to move forward.

In my experience, people can recognize this resistance because there is neither a desire to justify nor a feeling of judgment or fear - just the knowledge that this process does not seem right for them at the time. It comes with a sense of calm. There is no desire to attack or run – just a feeling of peace and confidence with the decision.

Remedy: The beautiful thing about this type of resistance is that there is no remedy required! You can state your case and then do nothing. If you've misread your intuition and change would be beneficial, another opportunity to do so will present itself quickly and most often positively. Problems can arise, however, when others work to influence you to change your mind. If this happens, stand strong without being defensive and this resistance will quite naturally work its way out.

Change will never be easy for most people, but becoming aware of your own responses and what they might mean to you can make it more pleasant.

As you read this book, take a deep breath, relax and notice how you are feeling. Enjoy those things that resonate and take action on them immediately. Avoid 'shoulding' on yourself by adding unnecessary items to your to do list simply because they sound exciting. When resistance arises, try the remedy provided. Sometimes, just recognizing resistance will make it go away.

If you can do this throughout this book, you will enjoy the process, pick up plenty of great tips and find yourself standing in your power in no time at all.

Meet Jane

"Jordan! Come and clean up the mess you made in the kitchen – fast! We had to be out the door five minutes ago!" My throat is already hoarse and it's only ten before eight in the morning.

"It's not my mess!" screams my ten year old drama queen. "You always blame me for everything – *Jordan you left out the juice! Jordan, you're making us late! Jordan you're screwing up everything - again!*" she yells in a high pitched voice, which I can only guess is supposed to sound like me.

Pushing past me, she yanks her lunch off the counter, stuffs it in her backpack and runs out the door, slamming it behind her while totally ignoring the mess.

I want to yell at her to come back, but self-doubt, frustration and uncertainty flood through me. They make me bite my tongue and wonder if I pick on her more than the others. She is the oldest, after all, and maybe I do expect more from her. Sighing, I turn to my five-year-old son and seven-year-old daughter.

"Okay, you two, grab your lunches and go out to the car with your sister. I'm just going to quickly clean up. When I come out, you need to be in the car and ready to go." I point at their lunches and give a half smile in case they think my frustration is at them.

"It's not a car, Mom," corrects Amy, crossing her arms and rolling her eyes, as if I'm the stupidest person alive. I'm sure she's learned this behaviour from watching Jordan.

Adam mimics his sister's crossed arms and drops his lunch in the process. "It's a van."

"OUT . . . NOW!" I bellow, wondering if Adam's fruit will now have a big bruise. Our dog, Tippet, a medium sized shepherd cross we rescued as a pup, jumps up and slinks over to me. It's as if she knows she is about to be beaten, despite the fact that she's never been spanked in the three years we've had her.

"YOU TOO!" I yell at the dog, knowing I'm scaring her. The thought of giving her a whack or two flashes briefly through my mind, but I quickly dismiss it as inappropriate.

"Go to your bed!" I order, pointing at her cedar pad in the corner. Not caring if she listens or not, I turn back to the mess.

Grabbing the almond milk, I yank open the fridge and stuff it inside. The little top pops off and the milk look-alike sloshes out and onto the food below. I look at the clock . . . five to eight . . . I'm going to be late for work - again! Slamming the fridge, I bite my lip and try to hold back the tears.

Why is this so hard? Every morning I swear it's going to be better and every morning I'm wrong! I didn't sign up for this . . . I hate my life! Instantly I'm plagued with guilt: *how can I hate my life? I have a great job, a good husband (even if he is away a lot), beautiful kids and a dog that loves me no matter how bad I treat her.*

Now the tears are really flowing. A mascara-blackened tear falls onto my hand; my make-up is ruined for sure. It's too late to do anything about it. I grab my keys and run out to the van.

check with CJOB
for "Your Life unlimited"

- Debbie talked to
Deb Dawson-Dunn
(getitdone.ca)

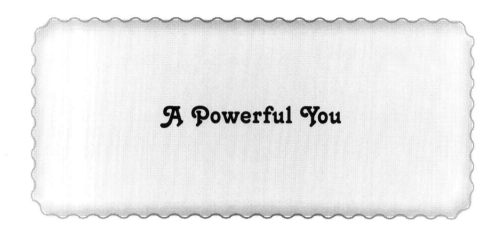

A Powerful You

1: You are Incomparable

What would a powerful you look like? How would you recognize her? Is there someone who comes to mind when you ask yourself this question? Perhaps it's a neighbour, your boss, a colleague, a movie star or a heroine from a book.

Some people see power in a person who doesn't take any guff - the one who is afraid of nothing and couldn't care less about how others perceive her. This is not the kind of power I am speaking of having. Aspects of it are part of our plan, but becoming pushy and uncaring is never our goal.

Before you can begin creating a list of qualities you see as powerful, it's important to debunk a myth that you've likely bought into.

Myth: Other people and their success or lack of it will provide a good measuring stick to use in determining success on your own journey.

This assumption is simply not true! Even though your journey may look similar to someone else's, it is never exactly the same. The challenge with such a myth is that you end up comparing apples to bananas and deciding that one is fatter than it should be, the other not nearly as juicy. Bananas and apples both qualify as fruit, but after that, the similarities are few.

If either of these fruits believed they should be more like the other, they would have to completely change who they are. Thankfully, fruit does not spend any time comparing itself to others, but humans definitely do.

> **You are incomparable and as such it is impossible for you to be better or worse than anyone else.**

For example, you might belong to a Mom's & Preschoolers group where every mother present has a child under five-years-old. The temptation is to think that, because of this similarity, you are comparable to them. But what happens when your child is the only one who won't listen when it's time to sit down and read stories? Chances are that you will do a quick scan of the room, see everyone else getting compliance from their child and feel as if you do not measure up.

Interestingly, you will feel better if you can identify extra challenges in your world: I'm a single parent and the others have partners; I have three kids while the others only have one or two; my child is being tested for ADHD which makes it harder for him to sit still. Of course, if you discover the opposite, for example, that you're one of the few parents with a contributing partner, only one child and no apparent diagnoses on the way, you feel even worse.

> **Your journey is unique. The opportunities you face, the people you meet, the challenges you struggle through are specific to you even when they look similar to somebody else's.**

Humans love to put things into groups. Doing so makes it easier to talk, to narrow things down and to make comparisons. There is nothing wrong with this behaviour until we talk about people and use these comparisons as a way to decide if the members of the group measure up. This kind of thinking produces stereotypes, discrimination, superiority complexes and many other kinds of negative behaviours, such as ageism, sexism and racism, so it's very important we are aware of this habit.

Every single human being is unique. They will share similarities with others and those characteristics can be used to put them in categories. But just like the apple and banana, that comparison does not dictate whether they are good or bad.

It hurts to feel as if you do not measure up to others and it causes all sorts of challenges when you believe that you are superior. Instead of buying into this way of thinking, understand that your measure of success must be specific to you as a person. You can use others for information, support and ideas, but to stand in your power, you need to openly embrace the reality that your measuring stick will be different than everyone else's.

> **You can look to others for ideas and advice, but in the end, you must tap into your own inner guidance to figure out what will be the best thing for you**

Accordingly, when you are thinking about how a powerful you looks, use others to help you find the traits or behaviours that you

...ut do not use comparison as a way to decide if you will ever ...up.

Taking A Stand:

Create a list outlining the qualities you see as necessary for a powerful you. Using three different colours, highlight;

- the areas in which you are already strong
- those you are working on but would like to improve
- those you do not yet practice

Put this list somewhere you can easily see it on a regular basis. Don't be afraid to add and subtract from your list as you refine your picture.

Jane

I really don't want to go in there! My mind is screaming as my legs take me into the school library. It's the monthly parent council meeting - a group I joined, thinking it was a good way to show I was interested in my kids' education despite my inability to speak the language of instruction.

When my husband, Tom and I decided to put our kids in an Immersion program, it hadn't dawned on me that our choice might influence my ability to be involved in my kids' schooling. Not that the teachers have ever told me I wasn't welcome in the class. But you start to feel more like a hindrance than a help when you don't understand most of what's being said, never mind how to spell or count past twenty.

So last year I attended the Parent Advisory Council (PAC); before I knew it I was on their board as Secretary. I thought it would be worthwhile to connect with other parents who had so much in common with me. We live in the same area of town, are mostly double income families, and our kids go to the same school, play on the same teams, and attend the same birthday parties. I thought I would have a million things in common with these parents. It appears that I was wrong.

These mothers manage to work full-time, coach teams, run dances, take language courses and have perfectly behaved children. I'm sure their houses are pristine and breakfasts always go smoothly.

For the most part, they are polite to me, but I can tell that they don't really 'get' me and I know they already talk about my five-year-old, Adam. He's had some difficulty sitting quietly in class during his six months of kindergarten and I've already had three phone calls from the teacher.

They want to put him in a special program that will help him read. I think this plan is just a way to get him out of class and give the teacher a break from having to watch him. I know that they don't believe me when I say I've read to him since before he was born and to this day, rarely put him to bed without a story. I hate that they blame me for his inability to read and that at five-years-old, he's already getting a reputation as a problem child. Putting him in a Reading Recovery program will only make it worse for him.

The Treasurer, Terri, a woman with a daughter in kindergarten and a son in Grade 5 with Jordan, smiles at me as I sit down beside her at the head table.

Before I can respond to Terri's hello, Rhonda, the Chair of our PAC, starts talking. "Now that we're all here – or at least all of the elected members – I think we should begin."

My cheeks burn. *How dare she single me out like that. Okay, it is 7:31 and we normally start at 7:30, but there's no reason to be rude about it!*

"Jane, do you have the minutes from the last meeting?" Rhonda asks, jerking me out of my pit of anger and into one of despair.

"Y. . .yes," I stammer, panicked that I might not have brought them. "I think I emailed them to you – didn't you receive them?" Flipping through my binder I wonder why I'd say "think" when I know for sure I emailed them. Silently, I pray that I brought my copy. "I didn't think I had to bring a copy since I emailed them out."

"Well, I would have made copies for everyone if I had received them, but I didn't. In the future, perhaps you could "*be sure*" to send them out earlier. What address did you send it to?"

My cheeks flame even hotter. My mind blanks and I can't think of her address to save my life. "The, umm, normal one," I can hear parents squirming in their seats and whispering to each other. *I should just grab my binder and leave, I really don't belong here.* As I start to get up, I feel a gentle, yet firm hand on my arm.

"It's okay," Terri says, pulling a sheet of paper out of the neat stack in front of her. "I received the email. It came last week on Thursday, which is certainly early enough. Your address, Rhonda, is the first one on it." Terri winks at me as she passes the copy to Rhonda.

"That's strange," Rhonda says, scanning the email and probably hoping I had made a mistake in her address. "I don't know how I missed this. Oh well, I guess we all make mistakes."

I want to hug Terri to thank her for saving me, but somehow I know that wouldn't go over well. So instead I pretend to be writing important notes while praying that my burning cheeks will cool down quickly.

Oh My Goddess! Starting Your Day Off Right

Your first thoughts of the day set the stage for how you feel and often what kind of day you are going to have. Notice the thoughts you have when you first wake up and if they aren't positive, change them, so they are. If necessary, create a list of positive openers and write them on an index card to keep beside your bed.

> Some examples of positive openers: I wonder what exciting things are going to happen today. My bed is so comfortable. I love my life. It's a great day to be alive!

2: You are Perfect Just as You Are

When people feel like they don't measure up, they start looking for all the evidence to support this way of thinking. In the next chapter, I'll talk about the things you might be doing to feed this drain, but for now, let's talk about how perfect you already are.

Although some people might try to convince you we are all here for the same 'mission', I have to respectfully disagree. As mentioned in the last chapter, every one of us has come here to experience a unique journey. It might be that you have certain obstacles to overcome, precise lessons to learn, a special light to shine or something else specific to you.

Not all journeys are meant to be challenging – which is why some people seem to get all the breaks while others seem to encounter nothing but setbacks. Part of our challenge right from the start is in seeing obstacles as setbacks rather than opportunities and labeling different ways of doing things as problematic rather than creative.

> **When you begin to recognize your skills, gifts and talents as something unique to you, your self-worth and ability to stand in your own power increases.**

There is no other soul on earth who is living the identical journey to yours. In other words, there are things you have been brought here to accomplish that no one else can do. This uniqueness doesn't mean you can't share what you've learned or that your accomplishments won't benefit others. It just means that what works for you may not for another and vice versa. That feature doesn't make anyone :r than anyone else or mean that our achievements are faulty.

Therefore, start to notice right now what your special gifts are. Often people assume that, because their talents come easily to them, they are not special, but something that everyone can do. This assumption is definitely not the case.

Taking A Stand:

Write down a list of the things that have always come easily to you; the things you really enjoy doing; any repetitive compliments you have received from others. This list will help you start to identify your personal strengths. By doing so, you will begin to recognize that you are perfect for the task of being you. Depending on how you are feeling about yourself right now, this undertaking may be challenging or very simple.

A Goddess gift: If you need more support to do this task, or find you want to delve into this area further, pick up a complimentary worksheet from my website (debbiepokornik.com/readingsignposts) to guide you through the process.

Jane

Crawling into bed that night, I keep thinking about how Terri stepped in to support me at the meeting. She's so confident! It's amazing how easily she managed to save me and put Rhonda in her place without making anybody angry.

After the meeting, Terri asked if I'd like to meet for coffee this week and brainstorm ideas for the fundraiser that we'd just been asked to run. I said yes, knowing I'd likely have to cancel like I always do, because of the kids and Tom being away so much. I wish there was some way I could keep this commitment.

Rhonda came over then smiling to ask Terri if she'd be able to drive the kids to swimming the next day. I was shocked to find out that they were buddies outside of PAC, and that Rhonda didn't seem to have any hard feelings towards Terri's earlier challenge.

"Obviously she has a lot more skills than you do," a snarky voice says in my head. *Yes she does, I murmur. Hanging out with her might be just what I need.*

Oh My Goddess! The Gift of Gratitude

A beautiful way to end the day as you get ready to drift off to sleep is to think about all the things you have to be grateful for on that day. They don't have to be in any order and your list doesn't have to cover everything. If you struggle with this idea, start simple and follow with whatever idea comes to mind.

I'm grateful for . . . breathing, the sun shining, my pillow, having my whole bed to myself, that the kids are sleeping, for my son's laugh, for my mother caring enough to challenge me on everything, for my back patio, for my nice toenails, for my car.

You Are Perfect – Now Let's Fix You!

It's possible, as you read through this book, that you might be wondering, *how can you tell me I'm perfect and provide a book on personal development at the same time?* This raises a great question and one that I must address before moving on.

Often when people think that something is perfect, they believe that changing it would be wrong. This way of thinking can trap them into seeing life as stagnant rather than the dynamic process that it actually is. So let me clarify what I mean by perfect.

A newborn child is perfect from the moment she is born. There might be things about her that you would like her to grow out of (perhaps her sleeping habits or making strange to her father); however, you recognize these aren't deficiencies – just preferences.

As the child grows, she remains perfect. Her silly moments, tantrums, and even her ability to push your buttons might not make her fun to be around at times, but these traits are a piece of who she is and do not make her any less perfect.

At the same time as you recognize this, you also acknowledge that, unless something is getting in the way of this child's development, she is going to grow physically, mentally, emotionally and spiritually.

In other words, this child is expected to grow and to change, but she isn't any less perfect now. This assumption simply suggests that growing and the change that comes with it is what life is all about.

To sum it up, embrace your personal development, be open to learning, unblocking and advancing yourself, knowing all the while that you are absolutely perfect just as you are.

Common Power Drains

3: How to Quiet the Voice that Keeps Putting You Down

The inner critic is that little voice inside your head that reminds you of every mistake you ever made and suggests that you are crazy to take risks or try new things. Sometimes this voice will sound like someone you know - your parent, a teacher, or your life partner - and other times it's an unrecognizable voice.

While most of us have experienced the inner critic, she is not a given and does not have to be present in our lives. Becoming aware of her voice is the first step in taking back your power from this invisible force.

The inner critic is **not** speaking the truth. It might sound like she is because of the memories she brings up, but she is not. If she tries to remind you of a previous mistake, remind her that mistakes are how you learn and grow. Just because you've failed in your past doesn't mean you'll fail every time. If this was the case, none of us would ever have learned how to walk.

Your critic loves to jump in when self-doubt, uncertainty, worry, guilt or fear are around as well as when you are feeling embarrassed, disappointed, hurt or angry. She is like a ring leader to those feelings, working to rile them up, making it even harder for you to come through a difficult moment in a healthy way.

Once you recognize that this voice is present and tries to stop you from succeeding in life, your next step is to figure out ways to silence her.

The following tips can help you quiet the inner critic:

Tip 1: If the voice brings up strong feelings, let them rise to the surface rather than ignore them or try to stuff them away. Close your eyes and try to figure out where those feelings are sitting in your body. Put your hand on or near the spot you've identified. Notice any thoughts, memories or pictures that come up and acknowledge them. Try sending love from your hand to that area of your body – as if love is flowing from your heart, down your arm and out the palm of your hand. Sometimes, simply accepting the memory, thought or picture that arises without trying to change, fix or let go of anything is enough.

This tip works to quiet the inner critic by releasing the hold that memory, and its trapped feelings have on you and by pointing out that you are releasing the need to hold onto it. If you feel like a piece of you is stuck on a memory, take a deep cleansing breath and recognize that you have made this memory part of your story. Even though it never was nor will it ever be part of who you really are.

Tip 2: When there is no memory or you just don't feel like trying Tip #1, another option is to go into debate mode. Stand your ground and point out every single thing you can think of that pokes holes in the story that the inner critic is trying so hard to sell. In debate mode, you

don't take things personally or attack someone else. You also
give in even if you have a nagging feeling your opponent m
right. Once reasonable doubt is created, the inner critic will natura..
quiet down. Winning that debate can literally change your life!

Tip 3: Use your creativity to lessen the power of your inner critic. Draw a picture of it and add a clown nose or Dumbo ears. Create a pretend volume button and turn it low or mute it altogether. You might even give it a Goofy or Mickey Mouse voice.

Another option is to see it sitting there on your shoulder and flick it off when it won't be quiet. The point you are making with this exercise is that you are a strong and capable person and your inner critic is spouting nonsense.

Tip 4: Another successful way to quiet your critic is to send her on a vacation. Help her pack her bags, buy her a virtual ticket and send her off. You might want to remember to make the ticket one-way. If you hear her talking to you after she's left, remind yourself that she must be a figment of your imagination and refuse to listen.

Taking A Stand:

Believe in yourself! Know that you are perfect at being you and that you are on a unique and special journey. Nobody else will ever be able to walk a mile in your shoes nor will she ever fully understand what you must do to reach your full potential. Tune out the inner critic and tune into your natural guidance – you're worth it!

Jane

It's ten to seven on Thursday evening and I promised Terri I'd meet her in the coffee shop at seven.

As usual, you're late the snarky voice in my head reminds me. *I wonder if she'll wait*, it continues, *as if she needs your help, especially now that she knows you're unreliable.*

I reach over and turn up the radio, trying to drown out the annoying voice. I'm excited about meeting with Terri, or at least I was right up until I realized I was going to be late.

I couldn't believe how perfectly everything worked out so that this meeting could happen. When we initially set it up, I knew my husband would still be on the road and my kids hate babysitters. I decided to pretend as if it would all work out. Instead of worrying about canceling, which is what I'd normally do, I just continued planning as if my husband were home.

On Wednesday, my mom called and asked if she could come and stay at my place for a few days while they fumigated her apartment for ants. Next to pizza, my mom is the kid's favourite treat, so I ordered a pizza, temporarily removed the kids' electronics ban and told my mom to come on over.

At 7:03 I pull into the coffee shop parking lot and there isn't a single parking space available. *Of course there isn't a spot*, the voice starts up. *You keep mistaking life for something that should be easy and fun, but what have you done to deserve that kind of life? Just because your mom saved you doesn't mean everything will be perfect now.*

Finding a spot on a nearby street, I struggle to parallel park then run against the wind to the coffee shop.

My phone says 7:09. Terri's at a table sipping something creamy and reading the *Coffee News*. She smiles as I weave my way over to her table, my apology and explanation already forming.

I catch my reflection in the strip of mirror behind her. My weak apology freezes on my lips.

Look at you, Snarky practically shouts. *Your jacket's undone and falling off your shoulder, your hair's a frizzy mess from the wind and you look like a deer about to be run over by a semi! If Terri doesn't pick up her coffee and run the other way, she's crazy.*

Tears spring into my eyes and Terri's smile fades. "What's wrong?" she asks with a genuine look of concern.

"Nothing," I stammer, fighting back the tears. "It's just, I'm sorry. . ." My voice catches. Snarky is going on about how pathetic I sound when a sob escapes from my lips. "The pizza was late," I manage to say, "I so wanted this meeting to be perfect and now I've ruined it." Rather than sit down, I pick up my bag from the chair, and start to turn away.

Terri's warm hand grabs my cold one and her smile returns.

"Jane, sit down," she says in a soothing and confident voice. "You're ten minutes late, not an hour and I don't know what this gibberish is about ruining our meeting. Nothing has been ruined. I love when people are late in meeting me at the coffee shop because it means I can sit here guilt-free without having to cater to anyone's needs but my own. You did me a favour by being late – although it would have been fine if you weren't. Why are you being so hard on yourself?"

Terri's words seem to open a flood gate. I'm shocked to find myself telling her all about the snarky voice in my head, how uncertain I feel half the time and how no one listens to me, even my kids. Tears run down my face and my nose starts running uncontrollably. I try to staunch it with my hand, but only manage to smear my cheek. I hate how whiny my voice sounds. Realizing a tissue is required, I begin pulling everything out of my purse.

Snarky starts in about what a fool I'm making of myself, but Terri's friendly voice drowns it out. I feel her hand turn my hand over. In it she puts a plastic pack of tissues.

Common Power Drains

"Listen to me," she says. "That snarky voice might drive you crazy, but it doesn't mean you are crazy. In fact, she's called the inner critic and everybody has one – or at least the potential for one. The good news is that I can teach you how to shut her up.

You are a wonderful, talented, beautiful woman and I'm going to help you see that, but first things first. Let me buy you a beverage while you take a minute to compose yourself. What would you like?"

"Chai latte please," I murmur. As Terri gets up, I see my reflection again in the mirror. The state of my mascara, wind-blown hair and streaky face make me decide that a trip to the bathroom is in order.

Oh My Goddess! Letting Feelings Flow

Guilt and worry are two feelings that rob you of the present by launching patterns of self-destruction and giving back nothing in return. When strong feelings arise ask yourself: is there anything I can do about this situation that I'm willing to take action on? If the answer is yes, do it! If it is no, welcome the feelings and your desire to change things, and then set them free.

You might do this by physically moving your body out of the way and visualizing the feelings flowing past; you could put the feelings into a boat, a bag or a box and ship them off. What's important is to recognize these feelings do not define you - they simply convey messages that you are taking personally. When you internalize feelings, you quite naturally make up a negative story to explain why these feelings are in your life.

The more you allow your feelings to flow through, the less stressed and self-destructive you will feel.

4: The BIG 5 Patterns of Self-Destruction

The BIG 5 are patterns of self-destruction so common in life that they can appear to be natural. When we think that things are natural, we also believe them to be inevitable. Rather than try to eliminate them from our lives, we learn to accept them as given.

These patterns start with emotions that tend to pop up when a person is feeling uncomfortable, especially when others are watching them. These feelings lead to automatic thoughts which sap strength and lower performance. There could be more than five of these patterns, but these are the five that I notice the most:

Self-doubt – Second guessing yourself, wondering if you are doing something right and assuming that you are not.

Uncertainty – Feeling unsure that you are capable of doing the task you have taken on and uncertain you've actually got what it takes. This is more a question of self-worth than being uncertain of an answer.

Worry – Concern that your inability to do things right will actually hurt others, for example, feeling as if you've ruined your child for life, or that your mistakes will destroy the business you work for.

Fear – This is the fear of being rejected as a person. Unlike a fear of spiders or falling out of a boat, this is a fear of ridicule, judgment, humiliation and failure.

Guilt – Believing that all of the above are your fault creates a huge dose of guilt. If only you would have practiced more in typing class. If only you could take that class, or have that coach. It's guilt that if you had done more, you wouldn't be in this predicament.

ese five common patterns drain your energy and make it
sible for you to do your best work.

How these patterns drain you:

- They demand your attention often when you need to focus on something else, for example how to operate a new machine or a tennis ball coming at your head.
- They wake up your inner critic.
- They pull up any limiting beliefs as if they are fact, blocking your progress and giving the inner critic 'proof' that you shouldn't be doing something.
- They sap your personal power and make you disconnect from who you are and who you are capable of becoming.

The BIG 5 are not a natural part of life, but are products of a society that judges, points fingers, is critical and uses comparison as a way to measure success.

Because we **are** part of society, we must recognize that it is up to us to remove these patterns from our lives, and those of future generations. Awareness of how you feed these patterns in others, as well as how you respond when these feelings arise in you, is the first step towards making these changes.

Taking A Stand:

Which of the BIG 5 do you recognize as problematic in your life? Make a point of noticing them when they arise and what you do to deal with them. One way to stop them from launching into a pattern is to visualize putting them into a balloon then pop the balloon with a pin. You can even make a game of this with your family by saying aloud something like; *Excuse me while I pop this self-doubt balloon I'm creating.*

Jane

Terri and I stayed at the coffee shop until 10:30 when it closed and then sat for another two hours in her driveway after I offered to drive her the few blocks home.

I was shocked to find out that she used to be in an abusive relationship and that she has been working hard for the last several years to take back her power and become the woman she is today.

She told me about my inner critic and suggested I give mine a name. I decided on Snarky, since that's how I referred to her anyway. She also taught me about the BIG 5 and how these patterns drain us of our personal strength making it impossible for us to do our best work. I had no idea other people might experience self-doubt too – never mind that I could control these patterns.

As a result I feel energized today, even though I was up way too late. Maybe the things Terri taught me woke up a bit of my own personal power!

"Good afternoon, Customer Service, Jane speaking. How may I help you?" I say brightly into my phone.

"Well, don't you sound chipper," says my mom. "Don't tell me your mood has to do with your mysterious meeting that kept you out after midnight last night. I wonder what Tom would think about this wild behaviour. You do remember you have a husband, don't you?"

"Mom, relax," I say calmly, speaking to both her and Snarky. "Like I told you before I left, I was planning a fundraiser with a woman from the Parent Council. We just got caught up talking about things we had in common. I'm not having an affair, but it was fun."

"Okay," she sounds only a little less suspicious, but if she drops it there, that's pretty good for my mom. "I hope you've made plans for supper. I don't mind helping out while I'm staying with you, but I will not take over all your motherly responsibilities."

"Yes mom, there's chicken thawing in the fridge which I will put on when the kids and I get home at 5:00. You just relax and enjoy the peace and quiet while you can."

Hanging up the phone, I realize that, for the first time in many years, my mom's suggestion that I might not be a good wife or mother did not flood me with guilt and self-doubt. Even more surprising is that Snarky isn't echoing my mother's thoughts.

Oh My Goddess! Are You Missing This?

Many people think of the universe as a place that we live in - nothing more, nothing less. What if, in reality, the universe is energy itself, flexing, flowing, changing and growing?

Try this little exercise on attraction: if you lose something that you really need back, clearly state what you need and when you need it by; for example, your passport within the hour. Then totally trust that you will have it within the hour. Forget all about it and focus on other tasks you need to get done.

Follow any sudden desires to put away your socks, sort through old make-up or grab a battery from the junk drawer. Before the hour is up the universe will have guided you to the item even when it's in a very obscure and unexpected place. If it hasn't led you to it, it's likely you are still trying to control the search or allowing feelings such as worry or distrust to interfere with the attraction. Trust and you will be drawn to it.

Celebrate your discovery and be sure to thank the universe for its guidance.

Why Boundaries Help Us Feel Whole

Boundaries are a hot topic right now and the more you learn about them, the more you will notice how important they are to being happy in life. Unfortunately, many people have been raised without clear boundaries and have no real understanding of how to set or enforce these bottom lines.

How you were raised, your level of self-confidence and your own understanding of what makes a healthy relationship will all influence your boundaries and what you do to enforce them. Personal violations in your life such as abuse, co-dependency, or privacy infringements can make you extra susceptible to having inconsistent and vague boundaries as an adult.

> **Fuzzy boundaries will rob you of your personal power very quickly.**

Boundaries are the outside limits - a bottom line that provides a border for what's acceptable versus what is not. A country's boundaries or borders let people know where that country's authority begins and ends. They permit countries to make rules and guidelines about who may cross their borders and what people within their boundaries are allowed to do. You will find huge variations in how strongly these boundaries are enforced and how clearly the borders are defined, but the boundaries themselves will always be there.

> **Mutual respect, a sense of belonging and trust all grow out of clear boundaries.**

Every unit of life has its boundaries: individuals, couples, families, groups, schools, organizations, communities, cities and countries. These boundaries are based on each unit's overriding values and are put in place to support those beliefs. They define the non-negotiable

- the bottom line that a person may not cross without serious consequences. A child who disrespects boundaries might find herself expelled from school, clubs or even her home. A citizen of a country who disrespects boundaries might find himself locked up, exiled, or in some situations, executed.

> **Boundaries are what separate us from others. Every unit of life has its boundaries – they help separate ME from US from THEM.**

Personal boundaries mostly apply to activities that involve our bodies such as eating, bathing, touching, sleeping, personal space and how we are treated by others. These boundaries are non-existent when we are born, since babies rely on others to do everything for them, but slowly build up as the individual gains mastery over her self-care.

As she grows, her personal boundaries expand to include a need for privacy and personal decision-making, allowing her to decide the path she will choose in life. By the time she is an adult, these boundaries provide her with an understanding of what she will and will not tolerate from both herself and others. It is important for you to become aware of your boundaries, so you can stand in your power and be sure you are enforcing what's really important to you.

> **Boundaries and the rules that support them provide limits and structure that help make our world feel predictable and safe.**

Boundaries are not bad – they are a necessity. They provide clarity about what is okay and what is not. If you are not clear on your own boundaries, others might cross them without realizing they are trespassing. Unknown boundaries are responsible for a lot of grief in relationships.

Your boundaries are a part of you whether you are aware of them or not. Figuring out your bottom line behaviours allows you to be clear about what you will and will not tolerate in your life. Boundaries help you feel safe, cared for and empowered!

A Challenge to the Feminine

Truly understanding the Divine Feminine and how it is different from the Divine Masculine is an area of study that is just now starting to recover after years of being devalued.

"Something big is happening for us women. We're on the brink of an evolutionary shift with the potential to alter the course of history. Millions of us around the world are feeling a calling to reclaim the feminine, and in so doing, to awaken our authentic power to co-create the future of our lives and shape the future of our world." FemininePower.com

At a time when women have made huge strides in overcoming obstacles in areas of education, career, standard of living and freedom from harassment, we appear to be at an all time low for life satisfaction. Numerous programs are being offered to help women overcome this gap between success and happiness.

On the surface, this gap looks like a group that is never happy – no matter how much you give her. Deep down, however, many women are recognizing that it's something much bigger.

What is going on? How does the feminine tie into this problem and why are people claiming – at a time when so much ground has been recovered – that it is still lost?

This is an area of study that could fill many books, and as an enthusiastic student of this topic, there is much I could share. My intention, however, is to give you an overview of some of the pieces that have really stood out for me, with the hope that you will explore further into areas that resonate with you.

5: Honoring the Feminine in a Masculine World

The reason there is so much unhappiness for so many people – women and men – is that both female traits and the Divine Feminine have been largely downplayed in an effort to create the society we have today. This situation has resulted in a major imbalance that has thrown all of us off kilter.

None of us benefit by blaming others for this circumstance; focusing behind when we want to be moving forward is a sad waste of energy. What's important for us to understand is that, because we have been raised with this masculine way of thinking, we believe it to be the right way - the only way - to be successful.

Talking about the male and female genders is different than talking about the Divine Masculine and Feminine. It is really hard to separate out the true differences, however, because they intertwine so completely and we have developed such strong opinions around these qualities over the years.

Whether you were born male or female, have undergone a sex change or are gay/lesbian, this section holds important information for you to read. Our cultural upbringing has had a huge negative impact on our judgement of gender traits, our understanding of the

Divine Feminine and Divine Masculine balance, the connection of traits to sexual orientation as well as the extremes we will go to in an effort to prove them all wrong.

To receive the information in this section you will need to open your mind, heart and ears. If what you are reading does not fit with your understanding and I've listed them as traits of your gender, allow them to BE without feeling you must attack or defend.

In all likelihood, there are pieces of yourself that you have learned to suppress, ignore, dislike and have worked to change. In some cases, you might have distanced yourself so completely from these traits that you simply can't believe they are part of your makeup. If this outlook applies to you, allow the information in without any judgment for or against yourself.

In other cases something that I suggest is a female trait may not be part of your makeup at all! This detail does not make you defective or disconnected; it simply makes you - YOU. You are perfect at being you and I would never want that to change.

Whatever the case, the Divine Feminine needs to be awakened in all of us. We all benefit by understanding what opening up to this quality means and how it can be encouraged. Men and women are different in more ways than just the physical. This distinction does not make either gender better in any way.

Read the information. Open yourself to the idea, process it and see if it makes sense for you. I would hate for you to miss out on awakening a quality that is stopping you right this minute from standing firmly in your power.

Qualities of a cave man:

The main task for men throughout evolution has been to provide, protect and produce. These tasks require a lot of planning, an ability to work independently and a focus on results. Competition, fight/flight (anger, fear), a need to rescue and avoidance of embarrassment can motivate a man to improve his performance.

Strength, assertiveness and even aggression are seen as assets to be respected. Men have a strong sense of accountability, are task focused and are driven by facts rather than feelings.

Calorie conservation is important, so if there is no obvious benefit in doing something, men will not do it, making them appear lazy and uncaring at times. A male's desire to stick to a plan is very strong as is his tendency to share his plan on a need to know basis only. It is common for a man to be unaware of this secretive habit unless it is pointed out to him.

> **The only way to rebalance the masculine and feminine is to open yourself up to the energy you've been ignoring. An unbalanced male must open up to the Divine Feminine in order to regain his balance.**

The male body is strengthened by using the adrenals (fight or flight response), so competition, thrill-seeking activity and intense exercise works well for men. The male body produces far more adrenaline than a female's body and burns it off easily with no dire consequences. The male body handles self-deprivation quite well and can operate successfully on broken periods of sleep; similar to a hunter taking catnaps while waiting for his prey.

The masculine is attracted to the feminine and has a natural desire to make his woman happy. If, however, a man has had to struggle to get his mother's approval or has dealt with a lot of rejection from the females in his life, this yearning can be an ongoing and confusing challenge for him.

Qualities of a cave woman:

Females were the gatherers back in the cave days and relied on the group to protect them. Connection to others was critical for their survival. As a result, the feminine desire to connect with others is a very real part of her psyche.

Women are emotion centered, meaning that our feelings guide our actions. We have an innate desire to please others, stemming from the need to be protected back in the caves, and are extremely adaptable. Rather than zeroing in on and tracking prey, like our masculine counterparts, we have diffuse awareness, which means that we notice everything around us. This quality allows us to multitask more successfully than males, but also results in us being more easily distracted and bothered by things that are out of place. Even a female who prefers things kept in a disorganized fashion, will notice when things have been moved around.

The feminine is about gracefully receiving and using pleasure as a way of energizing and balancing herself. This pleasure might come from movement, food, touch, relationship, shared laughter or creative expression. She gets 'filled up' by doing things for pleasure rather than results.

She is the nurturer and gains strength through creativity, compassion, connectedness and caress.

Women might enjoy the feeling of adrenaline surging through their bodies, but the female body was never intended to use a lot of it. As a result, our adrenals produce much less adrenaline, become exhausted much sooner and our bodies struggle to burn the excess of the resulting hormone from our system. As a result, adrenal fatigue is becoming a very common problem for women, leaving them exhausted and more susceptible to illness.

In sum, it is the feminine that opens us up to receive, fully engage in pleasure, create powerful relationships with others, collaborate and use our creativity to grow as a culture.

What imbalance looks like:

Women have used their ability to adapt to what is valued by society in an effort to push their way out of an oppressed state and prove they are every bit as capable as men. As a result, in masculine-dominated cultures, we have pushed aside and downplayed the feminine, adopting the masculine traits of independence, strength, production and competition.

The 'softer' feminine side has been labeled as weak and undesirable (except perhaps in private), and although tolerated in certain situations, it is neither rewarded nor sought after in the workplace.

For this reason, the relationship between men and women has suffered. Women are now competing with men rather than enjoying what the man has been programmed to provide. We shirk the notion of needing a man's protection and scoff at his secretive plans.

The woman has closed herself off to needing help, taking pleasure from things that do not provide results and being open to receiving. Competition between women has skyrocketed, making what was once a supportive, life sustaining structure for women into a dangerous environment filled with judgment, jealousy, manipulation and undermining.

Recognition of creativity as important to our culture has been pushed aside as 'fluff' and an open display of emotions (except anger which is needed for fight or flight) has been identified as problematic.

As a result, women are out of balance with themselves, their partners and the critical support of other women. In an effort to excel as parents, they are trying to nurture from a masculine facts-over-feelings point of view.

Some people have so totally disconnected from the Divine Feminine that they lack compassion, any ability to collaborate or work well with others and wouldn't know how to nurture if their life depended on it. These people often carry a lot of unprocessed emotional energy which they release in hurtful, often sexual, abusive and violent behaviour towards others, most often women.

Some men who are more balanced in the masculine/feminine still have no idea how to please the women in their life because their connection to all women has become confusing and competitive.

It is critical that we recognize this problem and open ourselves up to learning what the Divine Feminine is all about, so we can embrace it fully in our lives. This will allow us to balance out the feminine and the masculine the way they need to be rather than thinking that one is better than the other.

The feminine ability to adapt has helped us survive through the years and is something to be proud of. Now, however, it is time to take back our power and encourage everyone to embrace a more balanced existence.

Taking A Stand:

Think about the above information and notice the things that resonate with you along with those to which you felt resistance. From these thoughts, create a list to journal about, draw pictures of, meditate on or discuss with a friend. The goal is to figure out the Divine Feminine as it relates to you. Notice memories, emotions and blocks as they arise, so you can explore them in greater detail when you are ready.

Jane

"Mom, where are you?" Jordan yells from the kitchen.

"At the computer," I call back, amazed that school's already out.

Terri and I have been putting this fundraiser together for over a month; working together has been a huge gift for me.

In fact, the only reason I'm working comfortably in my home office today is that Terri convinced me to talk to my boss about alternating my Thursday evening and Saturday shifts so that I would be off one of them each week. I honestly believed that there was no way he would agree and I'd be fired as soon as I opened my mouth. As it turns out, there is some flexibility in the hours that full-time staff can work because our branch has such long hours.

That's not the only thing that has changed since Terri's been around. I've also met some of the teachers at the school again and discovered that they are quite friendly and open to having parents in the classroom. In the younger grades, they often give directions in French then say key words in English for the parent volunteer and in the older classes they ask your child to help explain to the 'English only' adults in the crowd.

I also had a frustrating, but successful, conversation with my husband about how much he is away, and what we can do to better support me in my role as a single parent. We didn't really come up with an answer, but just talking about it lifted a weight off my shoulders. Having my husband acknowledge that it wasn't fair to make me do everything on my own was even better.

As a result of that conversation, I joined a neighbourhood carpool. That means I drive the kids to and from school only two days a week. My husband was dead set against this idea before our talk. He kept stating, "The plan was for you to take a job that would allow you to drive the kids as needed," but he now seems to recognize that the plan was faulty.

These two little changes allow me to have a much more relaxing morning three days a week and to have the afternoon all to myself every second Thursday. I feel happier, our home environment is more relaxed and even Jordan is smiling more.

"Mom, I need your help," Jordan gushes. She walks into the room and perches on the edge of the loveseat. "I have to do a presentation on how girls have been mistreated and made to feel bad about themselves for health class. Ms. Roberts says things need to change, and the only way they will is if we girls band together and make it happen. She said it might be a good mother-daughter project, so you would learn too. Even the boys can work with their moms."

For a brief second, I wonder if Ms. Roberts is suggesting that I'm lacking as a woman. Then I remember mentioning to her that I would love to have some activities that Jordan and I could do together. Thankful that I didn't spin off into a pattern of self-destruction, I take a deep belly breath and silently recite my mantra, *I'm a work in progress and getting better and better every day.*

Looking at Jordan's face, I'm filled with the sense that this is the perfect project for the two of us to work on.

"Sounds like fun," I say, smiling at my daughter. "How about if we start it right after supper?"

Oh My Goddess! A Feminine Dance

Females need movement, touch and a regular release of emotions. One of my favorite types of physical movement is a Canadian-created exercise program called Bellyfit. It combines belly dance, African dance, Bhangra and Bollywood for an aerobic workout, then uses Pilates and yoga to stretch out and strengthen the core. It connects to the deep primal feminine within and is created specifically for women. Find out more at www.bellyfit.ca

Zumba, hip hop, waltzing or swaying your hips a little more can have similar benefits as can dancing with wild abandon or simply walking barefoot down a beach. Find movements that you like and feel that feminine energy awaken!

6: Reconnecting With Your Feminine Side

Opening up to the Divine Feminine is a very personal and wonderful experience. Even if you are a man reading this book, there are major benefits to reconnecting with your feminine side and learning how to release the limiting beliefs that hold you back from living in a balanced state.

Remember that it is the feminine side that opens you up to receive, fully engage in pleasure, build powerful relationships with others, be compassionate and release your optimal creativity. It's worthwhile for all of us, male and female alike, to know how to do this.

There is no fixed way to start making this reconnection, as we are all in different places in our journey. The ideas below provide possible starting points; decide which areas resonate with you the most and give them a try. Resources are offered at the end of the book should you want to take things further.

Recognize your emotions

The female is emotion-centered, so a major step towards reconnecting to the feminine is allowing yourself to feel. When you deny what you are feeling, you cut yourself off from your own message system! On rare occasions, this behaviour can help you get through a situation, but over time it damages and disconnects you from your inner wisdom.

Rather than trying to stuff your feelings or pretend they don't exist, welcome them to move through you. This process is not the same as feeding your feelings with negative thoughts, which only increases the emotion and makes you feel justified when you overreact. If you allow them, your thoughts will naturally match what you've been taught that these feelings reveal. For example, if you feel angry, your thoughts will provide justification as to why you should be angry - even if you have to make up the thoughts!

> **Remove your judge's wig and put on your investigator's cap. Curiosity about a feeling can allow you to notice it without trying to control, justify or push it away.**

The more you can assess this feeling from a detached, third person perspective, the easier it will be for you to have a conversation about it without getting caught up in the feeling.

Sometimes your emotions will guide you to uncover deeper problems – patterns you are creating in your life. By allowing yourself to feel the emotion, you allow it to flow rather than become trapped in a damaging pattern deep within you.

Physical touch

Physical touch is extremely important to the feminine as it awakens the senses, strengthens us and helps put us back in our body.

Many of us have been taught to recognize all touch as being sexual and to be very careful about allowing others to touch us. Touch can be sensual without being sexual at all.

Touch is rejuvenating, and while you wouldn't want a person with ill intentions rubbing your back, a total stranger giving you a massage can help you reconnect. Massages, foot rubs, back pummeling, hugs, caresses and stroking your hair can all qualify.

Note: If you really dislike being touched, I urge you to explore it anyway. While you might dislike the touch of another person, pulling a blanket tightly around you and being embraced in its loving cocoon can be the perfect touch for you. If you can't find any touch that works, then exploring the other senses might result in a happy compromise.

Connect and Collaborate

Part of the Divine Feminine is connection and collaboration; as a result, these traits can help to rebalance us all.

Connecting with others and having significant people in your life is an absolute must for women. We were never meant to stand alone and you'll find that you can do more, easier, faster and better by connecting with others. Although women can compete with others effectively, connection through collaboration is what strengthens us.

> **Cut out or at least downplay the competitive aspects in your life. Do this at home, at work, with your neighbours, at your exercise class, at school . . . everywhere you go.**

Try to look at things from a collaborative point of view *How can we best work together for the good of the whole?* Recognize the value of building your relationships. Courses on communication, conflict resolution, effective networking and brainstorming together can all be helpful in this regard.

You do not need to be friends with everybody, but you can be friendly to everyone. So once again, remove your judge's wig and put on your investigator's cap. Coming at things from this perspective is a big jump for many of us, but it's a jump that's worth taking.

The Pleasure of Movement

Movement is extremely important to the female body and helps to keep feminine energy flowing. If you feel stuck and need a refresher, find a corner for yourself and dance, sway or reconnect with Mother Earth.

If you are walking, sway your hips a little more than you normally would; creative energy gets trapped in the hips, so this little movement can make a big difference. The flowing skirts worn by gypsies in the movies and the jingle belts of belly dancers are excellent pieces to wear to help you to notice your hips and want to move them.

Another wonderful way of awakening your body and reconnecting with the feminine is to remove your shoes and walk barefoot on the earth. Take a walk down a sandy beach, across a lawn or down a dirt path. It's not great for freshly polished toenails, but the other benefits you will experience are worth it.

Create, Create, Create

Creativity flows from the feminine and allows the feminine to flow. Take risks and try new endeavours. If you've always liked to sing, play an instrument, draw or paint, but have been told it's a waste of time or you're not good enough at it, erase that memory and do it now!

Create new things - those that may or may not have been thought of before. There are no bounds to what you can create when you believe in yourself and are willing to dream.

Remember that you are creating for the pleasure of it. The results are not important although you will likely be amazed by them.

Tap into Your Intuition

Listen to your intuition. Pay attention when you know something is right, or feel strongly that you should go somewhere or avoid something. I'll talk more about this topic in a later chapter, but for now, understand this is an important part of reconnecting to yourself.

Open Yourself up to Receive

Opening up to receiving from others sounds so simple, yet it is difficult for most women to do. Allow others to help you, give you things and look after you. This acceptance is not a sign of weakness, but because we've adopted the masculine model, it can feel like one.

Women are meant to work in groups and to watch out for each other. They are not meant to do this alone.

The inner critic will often get in the way and try to tell you that you are not worthy. You are worthy and deserving just because you are here! The ego will try to make you fret about what society thinks of you for allowing yourself to receive and enjoy things for the pure pleasure they will bring. Your ego is wrong!

Until you are able to receive gracefully and joyfully, you will struggle to become balanced. Write down a list of all the things you would like to receive and notice when you decline something that's offered. Open yourself up to receiving and see what comes in.

Fill Yourself Up First

Right on the heels of opening up to receiving is taking the time to look after yourself first. I refer to this as filling yourself up and some examples of it are: taking time for yourself, getting enough sleep, dancing, singing, laughing and feeling loved. In Chapter 16 I share other ideas on how you might fill yourself up. For now, I just want you to understand that this is an important part of reconnecting to the feminine.

Pleasure fills us up. If you go out for an evening with friends and come home feeling tired and depleted, it's time to find new friends. On the other hand, if you spend time with a friend and come home feeling pumped up and happy, then that connection is worth its weight in gold. Start to recognize the things that fill you and help you recharge.

Part of the role of the female is nurturing others. That means the people in your family will come to you to be recharged. You can see this task as an unfair drain on your resources, or you can recognize it as part of the feminine role.

> **Once you are full, recognize that others will want to tap into your energy too.**

Notice colleagues, friends and neighbours who exhaust you when you see them. These people are depleting you without giving anything back. Limiting your exposure to them is a good idea.

The female is not strengthened through deprivation, like fasts, overwork or extreme exercise. It's okay to be healthy and fit, but be sure it makes you feel stronger in more ways than just the physical. Insist on time for self-care and avoid martyring yourself for the family. You will find your family is happier when you are feeling strong.

Jane

Out of breath, I flop on the couch. My stomach is sore from laughing, yet I can't stop the next giggle as my two younger children continue with their silly dance. Jordan giggles beside me and casually flips one leg over my knees. For the first time in years, I feel totally and genuinely happy.

A powerful feeling of love surges through me and suddenly tears stream down my face. At first I want to wipe them away before the kids see them and think I'm upset. But they feel so good and something tells me I don't need to hide. Glancing at Jordan I see she has tears on her face too. She catches my eye and we laugh even harder.

Oh My Goddess! Breathing for Hormones

Place one hand on your chest and one on your belly. Notice where the air is going when you breathe in. Breathing into the chest tells the body that you are in flight or fight mode, which means that you are in trouble and it is not safe to rest.

When you breathe into the belly, like a baby does automatically, you tell your body that all is good so you can relax and repair. This action changes the hormones that are being released and has a huge positive effect on your health.

For this reason, take a moment every day to notice how you breathe. Breathe deeply but naturally, allowing your abdomen to move with the breath. Take this even further by letting yourself sigh freely on the exhale. Make a contented, relaxed sound as you exhale and feel your body shift into a state that recharges and fills you.

How the Divine Feminine Can Help Us

Have you ever worked in a corporation where the staff is pitted against each other in an effort to make them work harder? People are compared on a continual basis and competition is fierce. It's a dog-eat-dog environment where everyone must watch their own back.

This is a common scenario in our society today and one that is not often challenged. Frequently, men in an environment such as this, will say that they'd prefer a group of egotistical males over working with a group of competitive women any day. This is so, because women are very creative, adaptive and tuned in to others. They are quick to figure out how to manipulate, undermine and hurt their opponent. Jealousy, backstabbing and vindictive mind games can arise, creating an environment where nobody trusts, feels safe or is willing to take a risk.

In such an environment, the 'tough' will survive and rise to the top, but only by clawing their way up there.

What happens though, if we take a similar corporation, only have this business value and promote a collaboration model instead? Assuming that their employees understand how collaboration, creativity and connectivity interrelate in this model and have the skills for working within it, what sort of outcome would arise?

A balanced male would have no trouble doing his best work in this environment and would enjoy the harmony in the office. He would take pleasure in the healthy and fun competition that naturally surfaces amoung colleagues with no fear of underhandedness or lashing out.

The women would excel as well. They would develop a strong support system with both the men and women in the company. They would work together, backing each other up and putting their heads together for ultimate creativity sessions.

The leaders in the crowd would immediately be recognized and encouraged to fully embrace that role. The rest of the group would feel nurtured and supported in exploring their strengths and improving their skills. In other words, everyone would naturally fall into the role that fits them best at the moment, while still feeling like an important and contributing member. No energy would be wasted on jealousy, backstabbing, revenge or undermining; all of the staff would feel invested, supported, safe and accepted.

Doesn't this sound like a great place to work? Hypothetically speaking, it is and this corporation would be unstoppable!

In reality, however, so many unbalanced people are struggling to understand why they just can't seem to find happiness that a corporation would be hard-pressed to find the employees who are ready for this model.

Interestingly though, if a business supports a system of collaboration and connection and if leaders are ready and capable of promoting this model, they will be surprised at how quickly their staff adapt or voluntarily leave the environment. Most people will feel the pull towards balance as soon as they enter such a place and will quickly realize that it's the best place for them.

This same concept can be applied to families, committees, communities and countries; if we are finally ready to start making changes.

Believing it into Existence

7: What Do You Believe?

The more I learn about beliefs, the more I wonder why we're not taught about them in grade school. My guess is that the education system as a whole doesn't necessarily believe or fully understand this area of study, so how can it teach something that isn't within its reality? But I'm getting ahead of myself here.

Your beliefs are ideas that you have accepted as real and adopted into your day-to-day living. In other words, they are the products of thoughts you've had over and over until they form something much stronger. Beliefs are extremely powerful, as they create your reality and actually have the ability to block out things that would contradict them.

Think about that for a moment. Your beliefs can block out things that contradict them! This means that what you believe can hold you back, help you move forward, make you feel good about yourself or cut you off from new possibilities.

What makes this worse is that many of your beliefs were formed when you were too young to even think about questioning them.

There is a saying, *"What you believe to be true you will prove to yourself 100% of the time."* I'm not sure who wrote it, but it sums up this idea beautifully.

You create your reality which is based on your beliefs. Becoming aware of your beliefs allows you to make changes in your life, fully embrace your personal power and open your eyes to all kinds of possibilities.

Many beliefs were inherited from your family of origin and sneak into your filter system without much thought at all. Some are formed through repeated thoughts; others arise when you experience something traumatic.

> **A belief is like a table with each supporting thought providing a leg to hold it up. The more you think about your belief the stronger it becomes, but start challenging your thoughts and the table will begin to tumble.**

Beliefs that are formed as a result of emotional trauma can be extremely strong - almost as if they are burned into your mind. These beliefs can interfere with your daily life; once recalled, they trigger strong thoughts, feelings and behaviours that were present when the belief was created. Sorting through your beliefs becomes an important task that is best done slowly or with an understanding that it could be unsettling.

Unless you do some work to think or feel differently, your beliefs will ensure that you repeat a lot of behaviours in life.

Taking A Stand:

Begin to notice the beliefs that govern your everyday life. You will likely have beliefs around food, exercise, sleep, bathing, pets and work ethic as well as religion, spirituality, relationships, skills and ability. Write down the beliefs you notice and take some time each day to reflect on where the major ones come from, what proof you have that they are true and how each belief makes you feel.

Jane

"Gosh, Jane." Terri is all smiles as she walks over to the table I'm sitting at in the coffee shop. "You are positively glowing – and here fifteen minutes early. What's up?"

Pride surges through me at her compliment. "I feel fantastic," I say smiling. "Things are going really well for me right now. Jordan and I started doing a project together last week and between that and some great information a very smart friend recently shared with me," I give her a knowing wink, "things are really looking up!"

A couple at a nearby table turn to look at me, an action which would have made the old me flush, but the Jane I am becoming smiles even brighter. Up until now, I'd always thought I was supposed to 'be seen and not heard', but today I'm feeling enthusiastic, so why shouldn't I show it?

"So is your mom back at your place or did you manage to find a babysitter?" Terri asks, blowing carefully on her tea.

I'm captivated by her perfectly manicured fingernails. They are always so beautifully done. "Actually, my husband, Tom is home this week, so he is having a pizza night with the kids. All I had to do was make sure the pizza was ordered and delivered by 6:00."

A strange look flits across Terri's face, then quickly disappears behind her usual smile. My stomach clenches. I want to ask about the look, but Terri starts talking before I can form my question.

"You haven't talked much about your husband with me," she said, "except that he's away a lot . . . What's he like?"

A picture of Tom floats into my mind and I see his strong 6' 3" frame and dimples on his handsome face. "He's great," I say. "A real keeper. He makes good money, takes the kids to movies, the zoo or playdates – when he's home, of course – and puts up with my erratic behaviour."

Terri's eyebrow lifts. "Sounds nice. How is he with housework?"

A tight feeling floods the lower half of my body, but I push it aside and respond. "He's a typical man," I reply with a laugh that feels forced. "He takes out the garbage when he's home, providing I remind him it's garbage day . . . and if we have people over, he'll sometimes help load the dishwasher.

Cooking, vacuuming and laundry are all beyond him," I continue, noticing a fleeting look on Terri's face again. My gut clenches tighter. "But I'm good with that. He works hard to bring in the money . . . My job, he jokes, is to fill up his tummy." I smile at the silly little rhyme I've heard Tom say since we got married, but for the first time ever, it takes an effort.

Terri looks as if she's about to say something, but instead takes a sip of tea, and pulls out her notebook. "I'm glad you're happy," she says with a half smile and clears her throat. "Shall we get to work?"

I want to ask her what's going on, but feel too timid to do so. Pulling out my pen, I open my book.

Oh My Goddess! What if I Were Queen?

It's a great idea to practice shifting your perspective on a regular basis. Use the lead "what if" to help you come at a situation from a different angle and see how it feels. This exercise can be hard to do when you're emotionally caught up in the moment, but the more you practice, the easier it will become.

Check out the ideas below and see if any of them help you see things in a different light:

What if the guy who cut me off is on his way home from the hospital after getting bad news?

What if my son got in that fight at school because he was defending his sister?

What if every time I smile my chance of ever getting sick decreases?

What if I found out tomorrow that I only had one week to live?

What if my child's messy room ends up getting her on the "Ellen Degeneres Show?"

What if every positive thought I have adds a month to my life?

What if my irritating colleague at work has been asked to 'test' me to see if I'm management material?

What if I only have half the story and it's the other half that will really help me to understand?

Playing these little games might seem silly, but *what if* they are what makes the difference between more good days than bad?

8: Limiting Beliefs

Do you believe all work and no play makes Jack a rich, but dull boy? Do you believe that being rich brings happiness? Do you believe that education is critical to getting ahead in life or that life is too short to spend it doing a job you hate?

These beliefs will shape what you think about money, work, education and work schedule. They will influence how you feel when you go to work, receive your paycheque, deal with colleagues and even how you feel about people like Jack. These beliefs will affect the kind of worker you are, your reactions to problems and how easily you tackle new tasks.

In other words, your beliefs shape your thoughts, which influence how you feel, which affects how you behave. This process creates your reality.

Limiting beliefs are those ideas you have about yourself that hold you back from reaching your full potential. Often these notions will stop you from wanting to try something new or believing you are capable of getting better at something.

> **Limiting beliefs stop you from reaching your full potential - and they are not even true!**

There are literally trillions of limiting beliefs a person could have, but here are some examples that you might be able to relate to:

- Money does not grow on trees; you must work hard to earn it.

- It is a parent's job to control her children, and if she can't do that, there is something wrong with her.

- It is the woman's job to ensure that a nutritious supper is served in the home daily.

- Lazy kids become lazy adults.

- The apple doesn't fall far from the tree, so if there are traits your parents have that you also picked up, it was inevitable.

- Red-headed people are emotional and quick to anger

- Taking time for yourself is selfish.

- Emotional outbursts are the sign of a hormonal woman.

- It's irresponsible to leave a job you are miserable at unless you have a guaranteed and equal income from elsewhere.

- Men have the final say in the 'big' decisions.

Challenging your limiting beliefs starts with pulling up and identifying the ideas you hold (often subconsciously) that are not serving you, but instead are holding you back in life. When you eliminate a long-standing belief, it is common to have it awaken all kinds of feelings, thoughts and other notions that have been linked to it. As a result, expect lots of little challenges to arise when you start making changes. Recognize this outcome as a simple, yet important part of cleaning out the system.

Taking A Stand:

Using the list you already created about beliefs, highlight the ones that hold you back or make you feel bad about yourself, and get ready to question them thoroughly. Start poking holes into the thoughts that have gelled together to bring this idea into being. Look for information that contradicts your original thinking, open your mind to new information, play with shifting your perspective and start setting the stage for changes to occur. The more you poke holes in the supporting thoughts around that belief, the quicker you can adapt things to support you on your own journey.

The more you challenge beliefs like this, the greater the number that will rise to the surface, so be ready for this to happen. Let the beliefs have their day in court, and then, if you decide they are serving you, let them stick around on probation. If, on the other hand, you recognize that these beliefs are limiting you from reaching your full potential, then walk away and replace them with new, empowering ideas.

Have fun with this task. There is no benefit in blaming others or regretting the time you have spent trapped by certain beliefs. Instead, put your energy into embracing the wonderful enlightenment and freeing feeling that comes from the recognition that you really are the creator of your own reality. Believe it and watch it happen.

Jane

An hour later, things feel good again and Terri is joking about how we might 'guilt' people into giving us money for our fundraiser. I laugh and feel a confident strength flood my system.

"Terri," I ask, sucking in a deep breath. "What was all that about Tom earlier? I saw that look on your face and it made me feel kind of uncomfortable."

"I'm sorry." Terri shakes her head and reaches across the table to pat my hand. "The last thing I meant to do was transfer my hang-ups onto your marriage. I think it was your comment about having to order the pizza and making sure it was there by six that gave me a bit of a flashback to my abusive husband, John. He insisted I have supper on the table at exactly six o'clock every evening; if it was ready one minute late, he'd dump it in the garbage and make me start over . . . or worse.

"You started talking about Tom helping out at home as if it was a favour to you rather than part of his responsibility. You were *joking* that it was your job to fill his tummy and how he puts up with your erratic behaviour." Terri drew quotes in the air in front of her and then threw up her hands as if in surrender. "I started judging him and seeing the red flags of an abuser."

"He's not abusive," I respond quickly, thinking of how gentle he can be with both me and the kids. "Although I do wish he'd help out a bit more when he's home and not have so many rules about how I should do things when he's away. I know he means well, but I just wish he would trust that I will do 'my tasks' and he doesn't need to check up on me all the time. I think he harps on me sometimes more than our kids with their homework."

"That's an interesting thought. I wonder if our kids feel the same way when we do that to them . . . I'll have to think about that idea further." Terri smiles and picks up her empty tea cup as if hoping it had magically been refilled. "Have you told Tom how you feel?"

"Kind of, but not really," I reply, random pieces of Jordan's research popping into my mind. "I did tell him after our last discussion that I was not going to drive the kids everywhere when he's away, and that I was joining a parenting carpool. He didn't argue about it at all. Just said that I should do what I think is best. 'After all,' he said, 'it's you who is doing the lion's share of the parenting'."

Terri's eyes are sparkling. "He does sound like a nice guy. Do you want to take a break from this boring fundraising stuff and talk about something called limiting beliefs instead?"

Oh My Goddess! Finding the Patience

Making changes to how we behave takes time, energy and practice. You must make this effort with the utmost of patience, similar to watching a child grow in height.

==**Being patient is about focusing positive energy towards the outcome, rather than being frustrated by where things currently are.**== Just like you cannot dig yourself out of a hole, you cannot pretend to have patience. If you scan your body and find you are fresh out of this virtue, you are better off to postpone whatever you were planning to do that requires this ability.

Mastering new skills and ideas is an ongoing, often time consuming, process. Do not despair that progress does not happen overnight or when, despite knowing about a skill, you fail to use it. Similar to many of our important life skills, changing your habits will take time, patience and understanding.

Be good to yourself – you are a work in progress!

Jane

It's 11:58 p.m. when I sneak into bed beside my gently snoring husband. Tom turns over and pulls me into his protective spooning embrace. He smells warm and soapy, as if he must have showered before going to bed and I breathe in deeply. His gentle snoring starts again.

Thoughts from Terri's and my discussion flow through my mind and I realize that tomorrow I'll need to have a serious conversation with my husband about family roles. Anxiety flashes through me. Then I remember learning that the physical feelings are the same whether I'm nervous or excited and how I label the feeling makes it good or bad. I decide to call this feeling 'excitement' and immediately feel a shift to the positive. I snuggle back into Tom's warmth and fall into a deep, comfortable sleep.

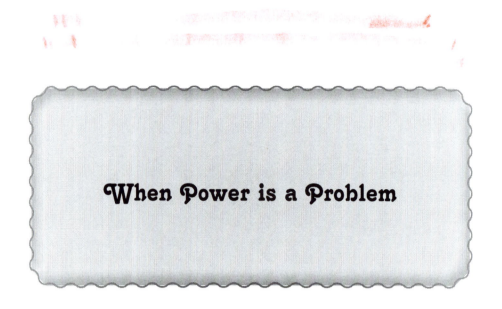

When Power is a Problem

9: Standing Up For Yourself Assertively

Standing up for yourself is an important part of reclaiming your personal power. It is also very misunderstood. It's hard to be assertive if you don't understand what it does, how it differs from aggression and why it is important.

Being assertive means standing up for yourself and the things you believe in without attacking or putting another person down. It is a skill that requires self-control, personal strength and clarity in what you believe. Assertiveness never involves behaviours like shouting, insulting, threatening or swearing.

When being assertive it is important to understand that this is something you do for yourself to let go of negative emotions. It is not about getting your way or setting the other person straight, as much as it is about saying your piece and feeling good about yourself in the process.

This piece is important, because if you think being assertive is about changing the behaviour of the other person and that person doesn't change, you can feel as if assertiveness has failed you. Anytime we try to control another person's behaviour, we set ourselves up for potential failure.

Assertiveness is a way of venting emotions that would otherwise bottle up inside of you and eventually surface as an emotional explosion or illness. The trick to using it successfully is to stay calm, make your point and then let it go. If you continue to rethink the scene in a negative way, you will not reap the benefits of standing up for yourself.

Although changing other people's behaviour is not the goal of this act, one of the great things about being assertive is that an ill-meaning offender is often counting on you reacting either passively by doing nothing or aggressively by attacking. When you respond assertively with strength and composure it throws him off balance which can result in a change in his behaviour.

Sometimes this type of reaction will create a reluctant form of respect, causing him to change his behaviour towards you permanently. When this happens, consider it a bonus to reap the rewards of your emotional vent and witness a positive result from your actions at the same time.

Taking A Stand:

If you are already good at being assertive, keep up the great work and be sure to model it for others, especially children. However, it's time to start developing that skill if like many people you have confused assertiveness with aggression or have been playing the victim while others walk all over you. Assertiveness grows from confidence which, in turn, feeds off being assertive. Notice how you react when people do or say something that brings up negative emotions in you. Take note of how you stand, the words you use, your tone of voice and, if possible, the look on your face. Self-awareness is the first step towards making any changes in your life.

Jane

I can't believe how good I feel walking into the Parent Council meeting only two months after my near meltdown. I'm ten minutes early and there are only a few people in the room.

Last Friday we held the fundraiser that Terri and I worked so hard on and it was a resounding success. We had awesome prizes donated for the choice auction, which I believe was due to our incredible assertiveness skills.

Sounds silly, I know, but the week before our event, Terri invited Jordan and me over to her house to practice assertiveness training with her and her son Nolan. The idea was to role play different ways to deal with 'peer pressure' which was part of the Feminine Power class project. Though the kids were resistant at first, Terri and I won them over by starting with our own goofy role plays.

When it was time to go out and request prize donations, we used our assertive skills to make the request and it was amazing what positive responses we received!

We figure that we brought in over $3000 at the event, but Terri is crunching the numbers and giving an official report tonight.

"Jane, congratulations once again on a job well done," says Rhonda our PAC Chair from across the room. "I knew it would be a success; everything Terri touches always turns to gold, but this really was above and beyond."

I still don't trust Rhonda, so I square my shoulders and take a deep breath, moving into my assertiveness stance. "Thank you," I say a bit more strongly than I had intended.

I'm feeling a little warm, but I look her right in the eye and continue. "We did do a bang up job."

Rhonda's eyebrows shoot up. "All that and modesty too." Her smile looks more like a smirk to me. She turns away from me then turns back as if she's remembered something else she wanted to discuss. "By the way, how is Adam's reading coming along? I understand you don't want to put him in Reading Recovery."

The three other ladies in the room look up at this comment and I feel my face turn red. *How dare she? I better put her in her place right now or she'll walk all over me from here to eternity.*

My jaw is tight, so I take another deep breath and raise my eyebrows. "He's doing fine, thank you. At least he's not getting into fights on the playground."

Rhonda's jaw drops open, her cheeks flush and tears appear in her eyes. I had heard a rumor that her son in Grade 3 was going to be suspended for fighting during recess. Because of Rhonda's position with the PAC, he was being put in detention instead. In an effort to stand my ground, I take a step closer to her. My hands are tightly clenched into fists and the thought crosses my mind that anger and assertion aren't supposed to go together. I push that thought away. *She had it coming and I'm not backing down now.*

Rhonda's mouth opens and closes a couple of times, but nothing comes out. Finally, she turns on her heels and heads to the door. Not thinking about why I need to say more, I call across the room, "Oh, I'm sorry, is that a sensitive topic for you?" She keeps on walking, but I see her shoulders tense and know I hit the mark.

The other women are all looking at me with shocked expressions on their faces, so I shrug my shoulders defiantly, walk over to my chair and sit down.

Oh My Goddess! No More Stuffing

Humans experience huge amounts of emotions on any given day. If you 'stuff' your feelings, eventually they will explode all over the place. Picture a cup filling with water. Once it's full, the water spills over the side. You cannot overfill a cup.

Instead of stuffing your feelings, become aware of how they present themselves in your body (tension, fists and upset stomach). Welcome them without attaching negative thoughts or judgment to them and watch how easily they flow through.

10: When Assertion Becomes Aggression

There is a fine line between assertively standing up for yourself and aggressively attacking. This is because the emotions that push you to stand up for something you believe in are the same ones that often cause you to overreact.

When you react out of anger, fear or embarrassment, you will often disconnect from what's really going on and allow your brain to feed your emotion rather than your needs. When you allow strong emotions and thoughts to fuel the fire, there is always a chance for things to rage out of control. This situation is similar to a dog viciously attacking someone when a tiny growl or raise of the lip would have done the trick.

Being assertive never involves yelling, threatening, accusing or bullying. Behaving in this manner doesn't increase personal strength or confidence, but allows you to vent in an uncontrolled fashion, similar to a volcano erupting. After your explosion, you will often feel ashamed, guilty, disappointed or resentful, as if it was the other person's fault that you lost your temper. This behaviour lowers you in the eyes of others making it harder for them to respect you.

The more you practice maintaining your self-control and recognizing when you are about to strike out rather than assert, the more you can keep the thinking part of your brain working for you. Clearer thinking allows you to stay calm and practice being assertive - half the battle when it comes to standing in your power.

Taking A Stand:

Self-control begins with noticing how different feelings present themselves in your body. When you are feeling sensitive, for example, your chin might quiver, tears might well up in your eyes, and your voice might catch in your throat. Anger on the other hand might appear as tension in the jaw, back or, arms, along with clenched fists, heat in the upper torso, scowling and a strong desire to yell.

The more aware you become of your body cues, the easier it will be to recognize when you are on the road to disaster. Choose the emotions that cause you problems; then start noticing and logging the body cues that come with them.

Jane

> To say things have gone downhill since my little battle with Rhonda is an understatement. Other people started pouring in for the meeting and the three spectators in the room seemed to buzz around to each one, whispering and making furtive glances in my direction.
>
> At first I felt totally justified, saying what I did to Rhonda, but as the adrenaline started leaving my system, I began to feel very ashamed. Of course, her childish comment brought our kids into the conversation in the first place, but even so, Zac's recess activities didn't need to be brought into the mix.

What hurt the most though, was seeing Terri out in the hall with Rhonda. I don't know what Rhonda told her, but Terri gave her a big hug. Other than a simple hello, she hasn't said a word since sitting down beside me.

Even the fundraising success was downplayed and the whole meeting felt smothered in a big, black cloud of unhappiness.

Our meeting was done in record time – just over half an hour – and Rhonda had barely finished receiving the motion to adjourn when she was out the door.

Guilt surged through me and it seemed that not a single person would meet my eye.

"I wasn't here," Terri says, shocking me out of my pity party, "so I don't know for sure what happened, but from what I've heard, you were pretty mean."

Dazed and hurt, I can barely speak.

"She started it." My words sound childish even to me. "She made fun of Adam! Besides, I was just trying to be assertive."

Terri put her hand over her mouth like she was trying to prevent any words from escaping and stared at me for what felt like forever.

"Do you have time for tea?" she finally asked, giving me a half smile.

"Sure, if you even want to be seen with a monster out in public." I meant it as a joke, but it feels kind of true and I can hear the bitterness in my words.

"I'll risk it," she says with a real smile this time. "Let's go for tea. I need to teach you about emotional control, being the bigger person and maybe even give you some background on Rhonda. It's best we deal with this monster while it's still close to the surface."

Oh My Goddess! Your Power Centre

When I ask women to stand in their power pose, they often do a superman stance with shoulders back, tummy sucked in and head held high. Interestingly, the power center for women is actually in our bellies. In many cultures, we have been taught to suck in our bellies, to do exercises to eliminate cushioning around there, to hate that area if it won't cooperate and, unless we are pregnant, never to stick out our bellies intentionally.

These habits disconnect us from our main center of power. The belly is the place where our 'voice of authenticity' comes from. Whether you are singing, debating or passionately discussing a topic, you will feel when you connect with your center.

The belly is also the area that grounds us. It provides us with balance and connection with Mother Earth. You'll find breathing into your belly, or imagining a chord connecting your belly to the earth to be a common practice when you participate in yoga, tai chi and other mind/body connecting exercises.

The very fact that the belly is the area where a baby develops from a fertilized egg into a little being with all sorts of body parts, should remind us that the belly is a pretty amazing place. Yet aside from pregnancy we rarely worship our bellies.

My suggestion is that we stop dissing our bellies and start loving them, however they look. Embrace the beauty and power that emanates from this area. When you're ready, stick out your belly and feel the power.

Standing Up for You – How it's Done

Some pieces of assertiveness, like eye contact and language structure are culture specific. Adapt this information to fit your cultural norms. Just be sure to maintain the strength of body and message.

The stance: Practice an assertive body by pretending you are wearing a cape and crown. Shoulders and head are held in a strong, confident position with the shoulders up and back, a slight puffing of the chest; the head is held high and proud. For women, the power center is located in the belly, so make sure your feet are firmly placed on the floor and your belly is not trying to hide.

Lowering of the head in a submissive gesture will result in the crown toppling to the ground, while raising the nose to suggest superiority will cause it to slip backwards, so keep your head in a neutral position. Hands are relaxed at the sides; clenched fists suggest anger and send a message to both your brain and the other person that a fight might follow.

Crossed arms can indicate defensiveness, fear or close-mindedness. Hands in your pockets are acceptable. If you do so, be sure to keep strong shoulders.

The face: Becoming aware of your facial expressions when you are angry, afraid, embarrassed and confident is an important part of being assertive. This habit is best practiced in front of a mirror, so you can rehearse what confidence looks and feels like in private. If you look aggressive (angry) or submissive (afraid) when you are standing up for yourself, things are not likely to go the way you had planned.

Your eyes are an important part of assertiveness. Be sure to look at yourself in the mirror during practice and get used to how that feels. In real situations, you can shift your gaze to the other person's forehead or nose if looking them in the eye is too much for you. It is not easy to look at the floor or up at the ceiling and still appear confident, so be sure to control those eyes.

The voice: the delivery of your assertive message will be influenced by how weak or strong your voice sounds, along with the tone that you use. You do not need to sound friendly, but you don't want to sound angry, afraid, sarcastic or condescending either. As a result, it's a good idea to take a deep cleansing breath before you begin talking to ensure that your voice comes out strong and true. Remember that you are royalty at this moment; use a voice that matches that confident authority.

The words: What you say when you are being assertive can either support or undermine your message. If you use attacking words, your opponent will often attack you back. Your goal is to get your message across and stand up for what you believe in without causing a battle or putting the other person down. In other words you will have to know what you are standing up for (your message) and practice talking about things in ways that support your message.

Starting off a statement by using the pronoun "I" can be a helpful way to stay on track. i.e.

I don't like it when you use that voice with me or

I believe what I have to say is important. Please let me finish. . .

Polite words (please, thank you and excuse me) are not required in assertive statements, but sometimes they just feel right. If you choose to use them, make sure they don't come out in a pleading way or make you feel angrier if the offender refuses to comply after you were so polite.

Other assertive examples:

> *I can see you guys are pumped about the party, so go. . . I'm staying here.*
>
> *I can't concentrate when I'm being yelled at. Please stop, so we can talk.*
>
> *I see you're angry, I'll give you time to calm down before we talk.*

The Outcome: Assertiveness is about saying what you need to say rather than keeping it bottled up inside. If the person doesn't do as you ask, you might leave the situation, go for help or turn your attention to something else. Whatever you decide, remember to respond with your crown and cape firmly in place, so your body language is supporting your message and you can feel good about how you stood up for yourself.

Jane

On the way to the coffee shop, I feel as if I'm having a nervous breakdown.

Wave after wave of despair washes over me. I wonder if Terri will want to be my friend anymore – if she even thinks of us as friends in the first place. *Maybe she was just being nice to me because of the fundraiser and now she'll go back to hanging out with Rhonda.*

How could I have messed up so badly? Everything was going so well, but who am I kidding? Nothing has really changed . . . I'm still the same bumbling idiot I've been for a long time now. I can learn new skills . . . but that doesn't mean I'm going to use them! Maybe Terri would be better off with Rhonda anyway!

Tears flow down my cheeks and I feel lower than I have in months.

Increasing Awareness

11: Practicing Self-Control

Self-control is not automatic, nor will it stick around if you don't practice using it!

We have to talk about something called 'the gap' in order to avoid those situations where one minute you're calm and the next you're saying words you regret or destroying things precious to you. A number of years ago, the late Dr. Stephen R. Covey discovered information in a book that he says changed his life. It was a very simple concept that went like this:

Between any stimulus and response, there is a gap

This concept doesn't really sound so life changing, does it? Yet in reality, it can be the difference between having self-control and losing it. When you are aware that this gap is always present, you can start to recognize that an inability to control your behaviour is more a belief than a reality.

You see, if the gap is always there, then you can always choose how you want to respond. There may be times when your choice is to strike out at someone, but in that case it's done with full awareness. In other words, while your response might be intense, at least it is done consciously allowing you to make better decisions and avoid spinning out of control.

Is the gap really there?

Imagine that there is a river you need to cross. In the middle of the river is a rock. If you choose to jump across the river without using the rock, it does not disappear; it simply wasn't used in that instance. The same is true for this gap. It is always there, even though you might not always see it or choose to use it.

Think about a time in your life when you were really upset with someone, but didn't allow yourself to show it. Maybe it was because you were out in public and showing how you felt would be too embarrassing. Perhaps you knew that reacting would put you or someone you love in serious danger. Maybe you felt that if someone overheard you, consequences related to your job, family or neighborhood would be a bigger price than you were willing to pay.

It could be that you started to explode when someone walked into the room and you didn't want to make a scene in front of this person. Whatever the reason, you stopped yourself from simply reacting even though the stimulus would normally have been enough to set you off.

> **The straw that broke the camel's back was no different than the many straws placed before it; the camel simply gave up its strong stance on the final straw.**

In every circumstance, the gap between stimulus and response allows people to use their willpower to control their reaction. This characteristic can even be found in abusive relationships where the abuser says they can't stop themselves from striking out; it just happens. In these situations, there are often instances that the spouse can recount when someone unexpectedly shows up, or others are present and the abuser is able to postpone the beating until later.

> **Events are neutral. It is our beliefs and thoughts about the event that give it meaning.**

People will try to blame the event for pushing them over the edge, but the situation is not responsible. You assign meaning to any event and what can seem like terrible or inexcusable behaviour to you will not always result in the same reaction from others.

Why does it feel so 'right' when I'm doing it, then so 'wrong' as soon as I'm done?

The brain does not have access to the outside world, so when you feel a strong negative emotion, the brain asks your senses if you are in danger. If you respond with negative thoughts and more tension in your body, you are telling your brain that you are in danger and a fight or flight response is necessary for survival.

The brain is totally in favour of staying alive, so it diverts blood from the thinking part of your brain to the pieces that will help you survive in a fight or a race. In other words, at that moment you have traded intelligence for muscle.

> **Allow your thoughts to feed the fire and you will get a meltdown or explosion. But take advantage of the gap by using your thoughts to cool things off, and you will be much smarter!**

If you want to stay smart, the answer is to signal the brain that all is fine and there is no need to fight or flee. When this happens, the blood continues to flow and help you think so you can keep your cool and still get your message across. All of this happens in the gap – the nanosecond - between stimulus and response.

Using the Gap

The trick to using the gap is to make it very obvious for you. Once it's obvious and you start using it, the more it will stand out for you in every situation.

> **Learning that tension in the body is often a clue that you are getting angry can help you increase the gap and take steps to calm your emotions.**

Since anger is the key emotion in losing self-control, body cues for this feeling are good to recognize. Noticing what your body is saying before you become furious or enter into a rage is critical as you have much less chance of regaining control in either of these states.

Beware of triggers!

Feelings or situations that launch a person into an angry outburst with very little warning are called triggers. These springboards to anger can include feelings like; frustration, irritation, annoyance, embarrassment, humiliation, jealousy, disappointment and fear. A short fuse can also be created by physical discomfort such as hunger, heat or thirst, as well as physical or emotional pain.

For some people a trigger can be a smell, a taste, a look from another person, a weather system, an unmet expectation or teasing about something considered problematic, such as glasses, freckles, weight, or facial features.

Becoming aware of how these feelings present themselves in your body and which ones will set you off is critical to using the gap. The more you practice using the gap and keeping the blood flowing to the thinking part of the brain, the more self-control you will experience.

This result is great for relationships, job promotion, self-esteem and almost everything else you do in life.

Taking A Stand: AEIOU

Aware: Notice how different feelings present themselves in your body and which ones are most likely to be triggers for you. Allow the feeling without feeding it negative thoughts to help it grow. Do not try to stuff the feeling away or pretend it isn't there.

Emphasize: Make the gap stand out for you. Find a word, saying or picture in your mind that you can use to grab your attention and emphasize the gap. Any time you notice your trigger body cues popping up, use your plan to freeze the moment: WHOA, Freeze, Stop, Think!

ID: Identify what you are thinking and choose positive thoughts. Your thoughts are the most powerful way to calm yourself and release tension which tells the brain all is fine and keeps the thinking brain operating. Positive thought examples: Stay Calm, Relax, I'm Okay, Breathe, I'm overreacting, I can do this.

OK: Anything that helps to separate you from the emotions that are building in your body will help you refocus your energy on self-control rather than have an explosion. Affirm your feelings and use your coping skills to calm yourself down. For example: in your mind, take a step back from the situation and see things as an observer; allow yourself to become curious about your feelings; tell the person you need time to 'chill out'; focus on the bottom of your feet firmly planted on the floor; breathe into your belly and feel yourself relax.

Use: Take advantage of your new calm state to decide how you want to respond. If in this state you still feel that difficult things need to be said, use your assertiveness skills and do it.

Jane

"First of all, congratulations on finding your inner strength," Terri says setting down her tea and taking a seat in the comfortable armchair at the coffee shop. "People don't like a pushover, which is why assertiveness is so important. They don't like bullies either – which is why we need to talk."

"I wasn't being a bully," I nearly shout, hurt that Terri would suggest such a thing, even though it's true. My eyes feel puffy and my nose won't stop dripping. I almost didn't come to the coffee shop, but at the last minute, I decided that coming here was better than going home. Several heads turn to see what I'm yelling about, so I drop my voice and put my hand up to shield my face, as if I'm sharing a secret.

"I'm tired of her pushing me around and when she starts making fun of my son and his reading challenges, that's where I draw the line. She's so critical all the time and I've had it!" My jaw is aching and my words come out in a hoarse whisper through clenched teeth. I was hoping, once I explained what really happened, Terri would be on my side. The anger I hear in my voice and feel surging through my body is a bit surprising to me.

Terri's eyebrows go up; I can see my little outburst has shocked her.

She purses her lips, takes a deep breath and blows gently on her tea. "So, why was her comment about Adam and Reading Recovery so offensive to you?" she finally asks, crossing her legs and leaning back in her chair.

"Well, isn't it obvious?" I sputter, staring at my tightly clasped hands in front of me. My knuckles are white in sharp contrast to my red fingers. My wedding ring is digging into my other fingers. "Reading Recovery is for stupid kids. She was making fun of his inability to read." Tears roll down my cheeks and I wipe at them in angry, jerky motions.

"Hmmm." Terri smiles a little and blows again on her tea, sending a whiff of jasmine my way. "Sounds like we've run into a limiting belief here about Reading Recovery. Are you sure Rhonda was being snarky? I mean two of her kids including Zac went through it. Last I heard, she thought it was the best thing that ever happened to them."

My cheeks feel flushed and I'm struggling to draw in enough air. "But . . . well . . . um . . . are you sure?" I say weakly, my tears flowing again.

Terri leans forward and bends her head down until I'm forced to look her in the eye. Her hands appear on top of mine and gently start to loosen my killer grip.

"Take a deep breath and relax your shoulders – they're trying to cover your ears. In fact, why don't you take a moment and check in with your whole body? I'm concerned you're going to snap in two." Her gentle smile and words finally register; I realize I'm pretty tense.

"There's no way you could have known about Rhonda's kids, but that's the whole point. Rarely do we know where the other person is coming from. Even if she was trying to be insulting, by being the 'bigger person' and using your assertiveness skills, you might have put her in her place, felt better and caused less damage.

"Adam's struggle with reading is obviously a trigger point for you which is good to be aware of, so you don't launch into attack mode every time someone brings it up."

Terri stops to sip her tea, giving me time to process her words. Realizing how badly I've overreacted and messed things up makes my mouth feel like sandpaper and my stomach hurt.

"As it turns out," Terri continues, "Rhonda was impressed with your efforts on the fundraiser. She knows she can be socially awkward sometimes and that she hadn't been giving you a fair shake. So she thought she was making friendly conversation about Adam and was going to offer to share some of her kids' results with Reading Recovery."

I don't know how it's possible, but my mouth feels even drier. I nod my head, close my eyes and wish I could rewind the day to about six o'clock and start over.

"As far as Zac goes," Terri says, her voice very quiet, "he's been bullied for over a year and finally decided to strike back. He wasn't suspended for fighting because the school knows what's been going on and decided he would benefit more by extra time in resource to work on assertiveness skills rather than spending three days at home. Rhonda feels terrible about it because she told Zac to *show a little backbone*."

I can't take anymore and a groan escapes from me. Rhonda was trying to be nice while I was hurtful and rude, going off half-cocked without the full story. I want to crawl into a hole and disappear forever. *How could I have been so awful?*

Terri's hands are back on top of mine. "I'm a monster," I whisper.

"No you're not," Terri says handing me a package of tissue. I wonder if she buys extra packages just for me. "You are a good person who made a mistake. If you were a monster, you would be laughing right now and developing your next plan of attack."

I smile at her words and feel incredibly grateful for Terri's friendship and wisdom.

"What this really provides," Terri adds, "is a perfect opportunity to replay the situation - with me being Rhonda and you practicing true assertiveness. Let's start with an I-message so you can separate out your real feelings from just getting emotional."

Taking a deep breath, I wipe my eyes, blow my nose and take a slurp of tea. The last thing I feel like doing is reliving the situation right now, but I recognize that if we don't do this, I'm likely to go home and replay this 'negative story' over and over until I go crazy.

Oh My Goddess! Relaxation - Just Do It

Yoga, meditation, tai chi and qi gong are all wonderful ways to connect with your breath, release tension, improve your health and calm your mind. Some people are afraid to try them for fear that they won't do it right, won't be able to quiet their mind or might be labeled as someone who 'does that kind of stuff'. If you are curious or feel drawn towards any of these things tap into the wisdom of Nike and Just Do It!

Meditation can be as simple as sitting in a chair with your feet flat on the floor, closing your eyes, breathing deeply and not purposely thinking of anything. If your mind wanders or panics, just allow the thoughts to come and go. You might blow them away with your breath, see them sailing past in an imaginary river, or put them in a helium balloon and watch them float off. As you do this, gently bring yourself back to not thinking about anything. Do this for one minute a few times a day and see how you feel.

12: Creating I-messages

I-messages are a communication tool that help you tune in to what you are feeling. They also help you recognize that you are not your feelings, and come to terms with why you are feeling a certain way. The general outline for how to create an I-message is the following:

I feel_____(feeling)_____because _____(honest explanation)_____

Notice that it doesn't say, "I am feeling." This is because it is hard to separate yourself from a feeling that you have assigned to yourself. *I feel angry*, is different from *I am angry*. Feelings are signals - they come and go as a result of what is going on around you. There is nothing wrong with having a feeling, they cannot and do not make you bad or faulty. It is the understanding that you assign to the feeling that you benefit by controlling.

In other words, you will naturally search for the meaning that feeling suggests when you feel something. If you feel angry and have been told that anger is a 'bad' feeling, then you will likely look for a reason to justify having a bad feeling. *He was rude to me!*

Anger is not a bad feeling. It is a signal, just like any other, and suggests that you feel that an injustice has occurred. Rather than search for thoughts to justify how you are feeling, an I-message asks you to think about what is really going on at the moment.

For example, you might normally say, "I'm angry because you always yell at me for no reason." But this statement would be inaccurate. With an I-message, you would want to go a step or two deeper.

Step 1: "I feel angry when I'm being yelled at and I don't think I've done anything wrong."

Step 2: "When people yell at me, I think they are blaming me for something. I feel angry that I'm being blamed for something I didn't do."

When you dig deeper for an honest explanation, it can totally change the conversation you are having with the other person. I've witnessed a situation similar to the one above, in which the 'yeller' responded, "I'm so sorry. Where I come from, we yell all the time - that's just how we communicate. I wasn't blaming you, nor was I suggesting you had done something wrong. I was simply expressing the frustration that I felt at the situation."

There are definitely times when an I-message will not get such a positive result and many people find this technique too awkward to use all the time. Begin to think in terms of I-messages and work to ensure that you find the 'honest explanation'. You will then uncover a lot of potential misunderstandings that, without the I-message, could destroy a relationship.

One final note: The best I-messages will avoid using the pronoun 'you' at any point in the statement. This format requires the speaker to release any feelings of blame or accusation from the sentence and take full responsibility for how she feels.

Examples:

1a. I'm angry that you walked across my clean floor with dirty shoes becomes

1b. I feel angry because I worked hard to clean the floor and there are shoe marks across it already.

2a. I'm insulted that you would make fun of my son needing Reading Recovery becomes

2b. I feel defensive because my son is struggling with reading and I see that as a sign that I've failed as a parent.

3a. I'm angry that you were talking to my boyfriend behind my back becomes

3b. I feel jealous that you were talking to my new boyfriend without me there becomes

3c. I feel insecure in my relationship with my boyfriend. I guess I have stronger feelings for him than I thought and am not sure he knows how I feel.

I-messages like numbers two and three illustrate how this process can help you identify what the real problem is and perhaps even an action that needs to be taken. You need not always speak the process

Increasing Awareness

aloud; just use the information to help you clearly figure out what is going on, what your true feelings are and your ideas on how to proceed. In both examples, you start out blaming someone else as if she is responsible for something she is not.

Taking A Stand:

Practice thinking in terms of I-messages even if you are not ready to use them in conversation. This strategy will push you to recognize what is really going on for you and where those feelings are coming from; it will also increase your self-control. The more you practice thinking in terms of I-messages, the clearer you'll be on how you feel and why.

If this starting point is too tough, notice situations where you do not use I-messages and later try writing some. Notice whether you ended up sharing what was really going on for you in the situation, or if it ended up being an argument about something else entirely.

Jane

Walking into the house while my arms are loaded with groceries, I nearly trip on Lego pieces scattered across the entrance way.

"I could use some help here," I call into the living room where I can hear music playing from a T.V. show I have clearly said the kids cannot watch. "Tom, if you are letting Adam and Amy watch that show, I will be very upset with you!"

The TV turns off and I hear Tom whisper something to the kids which makes Adam giggle.

"Come on, Adam," Tom says loudly to our five-year-old. "Let's go carry in those heavy groceries for your mother."

"Jordan and Amy are perfectly capable of helping too," I snap at him. "Just because they're girls doesn't mean they don't have muscles."

Tom walks around the corner, setting Adam down and looking at me curiously. "Jordan's at her music lesson and Amy needed some quiet time, so she's reading in her room right now. What's up with you?"

Right . . . I forgot about Jordan's lesson. I think about telling him that he should back me up about our kids' TV viewing and that I'm tired and hungry and the grocery store was super busy and there's no reason he couldn't have done the groceries if he was home all day. But my throat chokes up and nothing comes out.

I breathe in deeply and blink to chase away my tears. I reach for the freezer door to get the ice cream in before it melts, and notice my 'communication reminders' magnetized to the front. Damn . . . I'm not using them - again!

"Nothing," I finally manage to say. I clear my throat and speak more strongly, "I'm tired and hungry and my foot hurts from stepping on Lego." I'm lying about my foot, but the words just slip out before I can stop them.

"Adam," Tom calls as our son runs out the door presumably to grab some groceries. "I told him to move the Lego before you came home. I guess he forgot and I didn't even notice." Tom reaches down and starts cleaning up the scattered pieces.

I want to tell him to stop cleaning up the mess if he already told Adam to do it, but I can feel the tension in my back and jaw telling me I'm angry; I clench my jaw even tighter and say nothing.

Adam struggles to carry three bags of groceries. I notice one is about to rip, but since Tom is standing right there and I'm still too choked up to talk, I just watch.

Increasing Awareness

"Good work, big guy," Tom says, walking past Adam and throwing the Lego pieces on the counter where I'll have to clean them up later. Adam smiles at his dad at the same moment the bag lets go letting apples fall out onto the floor.

They look at each other and laugh just as I shout. "Oh, for crying out loud, you're bruising all the fruit!" Both heads turn to look at me with shocked expressions.

"It was an accident Mom," Adam says, his bottom lip trembling, "I'm sorry."

At the risk of hyperventilating, I take another deep breath and close my eyes, but tears sneak out anyway.

"Never mind . . . I know it was an accident, but apparently, I'm fresh out of patience and need a time out. Please put away the groceries. I'm going to my room!" Turning on my heels, I nearly trip on the dog cowering beside me and hurry down the hall before anyone says anything that might cause me to totally explode.

Oh My Goddess! Healthy Venting

There are quite a few ways to release emotion without taking them out on other people. Laughing, talking, crying, singing, dancing and running are all possible alternatives to yelling or attacking. Which ones would you prefer to use in your life?

For great information on why it's so easy to yell at your loved ones (even when you're not really a 'yeller'), pick up my free download at: http://www.debbiepokornik.com/parenting/nrg-boost-sign-up/

How Expectations Become Irreconcilable Differences

The relationship between life partners is a critical one for standing in your power. A lot of testing and boundary creation is done in this setting because often the people you are closest to push you to do your best growing.

When you were young, your caregivers made the rules and set the boundaries that you had to live by within their home.

These boundaries have a huge effect on your beliefs about what you can and can't do as an adult in regard to food, touch, privacy, language and arguments. They also encompass gender roles, emotional expression, sleep schedules and parenting. You can change these beliefs, but first you have to be aware of them.

Unfortunately, many people were raised in homes where boundaries were too rigid and restrictive, barely existent, unpredictable or totally unhealthy. As a result, when they become adults they feel confused about how to question things that don't feel right, how to put their foot down about things they will not tolerate, or even what's within their right to insist on and not be seen as selfish.

When it comes to relationships, one of the greatest gifts you can give each other is to know your boundaries and to share your expectations about them clearly and positively. It sounds like such a simple task, but it can backfire for many reasons, depending on your communication skills.

The first batch of problems arises from some differences between the feminine love of connection and the masculine need for secrecy.

The feminine love of sharing thoughts and feelings, coupled with a common history of not being heard, often results in a desire to think aloud. Thinking aloud tends to be circular in nature; this inclination can be extremely frustrating and confusing for a listener who just wants the bottom line.

When the woman tries to spontaneously share her expectations, she will often put out an idea, rethink it aloud, contradict the idea, share some more and muddy the waters completely before ever getting to her final thoughts on the issue.

For example: *"It bothers me when you call right before I'm expecting you for supper to say you'll be late. I realize you don't always know when you're going to be late, especially when traffic causes the problem, but I wish you could let me know ahead of time. Maybe you could call on your cell if it's traffic, but that doesn't really matter because by then, I've already started the meal and really can't do much about it. I guess I could wait and make the meal when you get home, but then I'm hungry and if you call that you're going to be late and it's not the traffic – there's no reason I should have had to wait . . ."*

This kind of conversation can work in a strong, healthy relationship, in which the man is content to let his wife talk until she's ready to provide the summary, knowing everything will be clear in the end.

When a relationship is already stressed, however, this thinking aloud comes out with an emotional undercurrent that creates defensiveness while it confuses. The result will often be an argument, hurt feelings, and increased confusion rather than clarity.

At the same time, most men like to keep their plans close to the chest and often aren't even aware they are doing it. To him, the only reason you would be sharing your thoughts is to get his advice or to have him fix the problem which he must understand before he can fix.

Add to this situation the societal message that talking about feelings is 'fluffy talk' and that, contrary to their tough exterior men need to feel safe to truly open up and share, and most men will want to hightail it out of the room as soon as their partner says the dreaded words: *"Can we talk?"*

As a result, finding out a man's expectations can be much like picking a tiny piece of eggshell out of your omelet when it's still slipping and sliding around in the pan. It's difficult to see, hard to grab onto and if you're not careful, you have a good chance of getting burned in the process.

As if that's not enough, there is another challenge for both genders in this type of discussion. Many people have been raised to think that, if they don't like what someone else is doing in a relationship, they should tell them so that they can change their behaviour.

This attitude feels like rejection, is unfair and totally ignores the reality – which is that people will not change something about themselves until they are ready to do so!

Telling your partner – *this is what I don't like about you and what I expect you to change, so we can get along* – is rarely well received or accepted.

As a result of the above, many conversations meant to clear the air in a relationship and share expectations will result in defensiveness, arguments, undermining of each other and, in many cases, a breakup. What started out as a desire to 'clear the air' and build a strong, open relationship has turned into irreconcilable differences that struggle to be overcome.

Jane

"Ahhh, that feels nice," I moan as Tom rubs the tension out of my shoulders. I relax more comfortably in his hands.

He seems to love giving me mini back rubs ever since I told him about feminine energy needing to move and how massages are a great way to do this.

"So what happened today to put so much tension in these shoulders?" he asks, zeroing in on one of the many knots gathered there.

"I think it was my whole week." I'm shocked to realize that only three days ago, I had the incident with Rhonda. Tom was away until late last night and I didn't want to share my story about what happened with him over the phone.

"I'll tell you what happened," I continue, "if you promise not to interrupt, or give me advice, or try to fix it or anything . . . with the mood I'm in, I might physically attack you if you do and right now I really just need you to listen." I glance at him over my shoulder, wondering if he'll stop rubbing my back and walk away.

His eyebrows are up, but to my surprise, he smiles, nods and says, "I'm all ears."

The story and all the emotion attached to it comes pouring out. I fully expect Tom to interrupt me in a couple of places, but he doesn't; he just listens and keeps on gently rubbing at the knots. "So that's what has given me such tight shoulders and then to come home . . ." My voice peters out as suddenly the Lego and grocery situation seem like nothing at all.

Tom continues for me ". . . to find Lego all over the floor, thinking the kids are watching a banned TV show and your lazy husband sitting on the couch, would have put anyone over the edge."

Ready to deny all he's said, I turn to him, but he takes my hand and smiles. "Just for the record, our show had just ended and I had told Adam to turn it off, but I whispered to him we should pretend we were watching the banned one to tease you. Not a good joke, I realize now and I really did mean to make sure Adam cleaned up the Lego before you got home."

The words *It's okay* are on my lips, but I stop them. "Thank you for telling me that. I was very bothered that you might be letting the kids watch something I asked to be off limits. I think it's important we support each other in front of the kids."

"Me too," Tom answers, lifting my hand up to his lips and kissing it. Tom's shoulders start to shake and a chuckle erupts from deep inside. "I know you're embarrassed about what you said to Rhonda, but I think I would have liked to be there to see it. Even if she was offering to help this time, she's been a bit of a witch in the past . . ." His voice fades away into laughter.

It hurts that he's laughing at me and I wonder how to tell him without causing a fight. I can see Tom is trying to stop laughing, but he's not very successful.

A vision of how I must have looked standing up to Rhonda flits into my mind and a giggle escapes. He's not laughing at me, I realize, he's laughing at the situation.

"Yup, that's me. Don't anyone ever suggest they want to help me or my kids because I'll put them in their place faster than they can finish the offer." My giggle moves into a full-fledged belly laugh and Tom laughs with me. Tears stream down our cheeks.

Deep down, I know it might be considered wrong to laugh at a hurtful situation like this, but the release of emotion feels so good and I've never felt more connected to my husband.

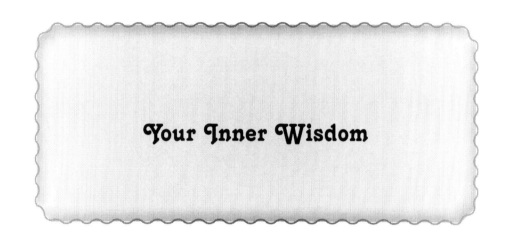

Your Inner Wisdom

13: Sharing Your Expectations Clearly

A healthy relationship with another adult – especially your significant other - requires an open discussion about expectations and boundaries. Nagging your partner because he's not doing what you need him to do, or suggesting he needs to change in order for you to be happy is not the way to create a strong home environment.

Relationship boundaries are a very important part of honouring your feminine energy. When you let others treat you poorly, ignore your rules or guilt you into doing something you don't want to do, you will feel disconnected from your power.

When you stand your ground - clearly, assertively and respectfully - you will feel stronger than ever.

Here are five important points to assist you in sharing your expectations in a healthy and helpful way:

1. **Be clear:** Before you even start such a conversation, you need to really think about what your expectations are, why they are important

to you, how you are going to share them and what you will do if these expectations are not met. It is also a good idea to think about and state exactly what you need from this conversation. For example, if you're looking for your partner's opinion, just need to be heard or want advice, say so.

You do not need to share expectations on every possible situation that might arise in your relationship. Instead pick areas of current concern and focus on them as they arise.

2. **Be gentle:** Introducing this discussion can be a signal to your partner to pretend he is busy even if he's not. A forced conversation rarely goes well; no one likes to start a conversation when backed into a corner. Offering a limited choice about when a dialogue can happen has a greater chance of starting you off on the right foot.

Is now a good time for us to talk about a couple of things, or would right after supper be better?

3. **Be brief:** If you've done your homework from point one, then it'll be easier to lay things out clearly and in point form. Unless your partner is partial to sugar-coating, which is very rare, just spit it out without all the fluff. I-messages can work well here although it might be hard to avoid the 'you'.

Example conversations;

I feel frustrated when I rush home to get a hot meal on the table by six and receive a call fifteen minutes before it's ready, saying I'll be eating alone. In the future, I'd appreciate a call at least an hour ahead of time if you're going to be late. If you do so I'll delay supper; otherwise, I'll make my own supper for six and you can make something for yourself whenever you get here.

or

> *I don't like the kids watching certain shows (name the shows) and would like to be backed up on this. I might be being overprotective, but I see behaviours that I think come from these shows and I don't like them. I'd really appreciate your support. In exchange, I am willing to back you up on rules you put in place.*

At this point, your partner might put out a different solution, explain something you didn't know about the situation, or simply agree with what you have suggested.

Please don't get caught up in the content of these examples. What I want you to notice is how the problem is clearly identified, an explanation is given as to why it's a problem and a solution is put forth.

4. **Be reasonable:** You got together with a certain person when the two of you linked up and it is not fair after the fact for either of you to decide how the other can improve. If your partner loves fishing and can't wait to get out to the water every year, it would not be fair for you to insist on no more fishing until your two-year-old turns twelve.

Being clear about your expectations means stating what you need in order to feel supported; it cannot be about changing the other person. Certainly you can ask him to fish less, but in the end, you must take action if your expectations are not being met.

> For example, *I'm finding it really hard with the baby when you are away fishing every weekend. I need us to figure out a schedule that we can both live by, or I'll be hiring a nanny to help out when you are away.*

5. **Be respectful:** Clearly outlining your expectations is never about threatening, giving ultimatums or being vindictive. In the first example above, you would follow through with your agreement and eat alone if your partner wasn't home for supper on time.

You would not mutter angrily under your breath while you sit there eating by yourself, scowl at him when he arrives home, refuse to talk to him or hold any kind of grudge at all. You were clear about your expectations and you followed through. Be content with that.

In the second example, you would not purposely undermine your partner's rules if you found out the kids were watching the 'banned' shows, but would use a skill such as conflict resolution to revisit the discussion:

I thought we had agreed not to let the kids watch _____ and to back up each other on our rules. What was your understanding on this?

Most relationships start out with the partners wanting to make each other happy. The clearer you are about what you need to feel respected by others, the easier it will be for your partner to choose whether or not to comply with your wishes.

Taking a Stand:

Think about a boundary you have that you feel is not being respected. You might want to start out with something that is not emotionally charged already; for example, avoid a topic you've been fighting about until you've tried the process a couple of times. Use the outline above to share your needs with the relevant person. Although the information has been shared as if the conversation will be with your significant other, you can use the same process to set a boundary with your parent, your teenager, a close colleague or neighbour.

If this strategy seems too intimidating at this point, ask a friend if you can practice with them first, or go through it with yourself in the mirror. Nothing will taste as sweet or feel as powerful as the real thing, so practice with the goal of taking a stand in real life.

Jane

Standing in the aisle at the grocery store, I frantically scan for a place to hide. My stomach clenches and my knees go weak. A second ago, I was innocently looking for 'dolphin friendly' tuna when BAM – I looked up and there was Rhonda coming down the aisle towards me.

It's been two weeks since the 'blow up' and although Terri helped me practice what I'd say, I haven't apologized to Rhonda yet. It's not my fault though; she's been away.

Staring intently at the can of tuna in my hand (as if I need extra time to read the three ingredients listed on it), I wait for my wish to be granted, but the floor refuses to open up and swallow me whole. My cheeks heat up, my eyes are spotting from lack of oxygen and the floor still stubbornly rejects my request.

I ask myself, what would Terri do? I hear her calm voice in my head – *breathe, close your eyes and breathe. Feel the calm spreading through you, ask your ego to sit and your higher-self to be in charge. Relax your shoulders and your jaw . . . keep breathing.*

A sense of calm spreads through me. Although my legs are still shaky from the adrenaline, I turn to meet the monster.

She's gone! I know she saw me and there is no way she passed by (we were the only ones in the aisle), but she's nowhere to be seen. A jumble of feelings surge through me - confusion, disappointment, relief, curiosity and guilt . . . I feel like the pinwheel my kids were holding out the window of the car last weekend spinning in all directions and wondering if I'm going to fly off altogether.

She's afraid of you. The thought flits into my mind, not like a judgment, like when my Inner critic says it, but more like a fact. As if on cue Snarky starts grumbling, *why would someone like her be afraid of you? Well, her loss. Maybe she's in a hurry.* But I know the first voice is right. I take a deep breath, recenter myself and head off to find her.

Oh My Goddess! Visualizing A Better Relationship

Nothing is more precious than your relationship with your loved ones. If you're struggling with a child, friend, partner, sibling or other significant person in your life, try visualizing them. Surround them with love at least once a day for two weeks, putting your hand on your heart might help with this.

As compassion fills your heart, you will likely find some of the positive qualities that person possesses start to rise to the surface, making them easier for you to see and appreciate (note that it is impossible to feel compassion and hate at the same time). You may also find your judgments about them or their behaviour shifting to a sense of curiosity. This awareness can allow you to see their actions for what they are rather than an attack on you personally.

It is common for your struggle with someone else to be based on fear of how they will be hurt or fear of how their behaviour will reflect on you. Think about this idea and, if it is true for you, realize that this belief is serving neither you nor your loved ones.

Compassion comes from a place of understanding and unconditional love; when these two pieces are firmly in place, there is no space for personal fears to interfere in your relationship.

14: Choosing Inner Wisdom

Not all voices in your head are problematic and good to ignore. Inner wisdom – something that everyone has – is there to help you, yet is so often ignored that it can easily be overlooked.

If you've ever heard yourself saying, *I knew that was going to happen* or *I knew something was wrong, I could feel it in my gut,* then you have experienced your inner wisdom. Some people call this intuition or gut feel, but the name is not nearly as important as your ability to hear the messages it shares. With practice, you can learn to listen to your inner wisdom and this voice can make your life much happier.

Your inner wisdom might warn you of a potential problem, nudge you out of your comfort zone, guide you towards a chance encounter or suggest a way you can strengthen a relationship with another person. In its simplest form, your inner wisdom provides guidance, helping you to recognize what's right or wrong for you, providing necessary warnings and gently prodding you to grow to your greatest potential.

When you compare this wisdom with the inner critic, things can get confusing. Both sources can be present as a voice, a picture, a thought, a feeling, or an image in your dreams. Both might warn you about dangerous activities, suggest new ideas or sound as if they are trying to help you fix a relationship. However, the resemblance ends there. Similar to identical twins there are differences between them and with intimate knowledge, you can learn to tell them apart and rarely get them confused again.

Recognizing the inner critic

- Often uses words that are judgmental, harsh, condemning, insulting and hurtful.

- Brings up past mistakes, builds on them and makes you feel bad for trying something new.

- Exclaims, sounds snide and digs for things that will arouse your emotion.

- Says things in ways that instills fear, uncertainty and embarrassment.

Examples of things your inner critic might say:

"You're a terrible person – look how you hurt his feelings!"

"What makes you think you could do this right? You screw up everything. Why would this be any different?"

"You left the cat out again. You don't deserve to own a cat; it's a wonder she's still alive!"

"The roads are icy and visibility is poor. If you drive in this weather, you put your life at risk just for a meeting!"

Recognizing your inner wisdom

- Uses nonjudgmental language and is unbiased towards the outcome.

- Information is given as an observation, a suggestion or as something to note rather than 'must do', although it can come with a guided action.

- It comes with no sense of urgency or emotional attachment.

- Doesn't make you feel afraid or even concerned – in fact, it comes with a calm sense of certainty.

Examples of things your inner wisdom might say:

"His feelings look hurt."

"Tell him you're sorry."

"Move the report away from the cup of coffee."

"The cat is outside."

"Look out the back door."

"Don't go to the meeting."

"Switch lanes."

The next time you hear a voice in your head, listen to how it's talking to you. If it's emotional, critical or biased towards an outcome; then it's likely the inner critic and she is not there to help. On the other hand, if this voice calmly provides an unemotional message without any judgment or concern, it's likely your inner wisdom and well worth noticing.

Taking a Stand:

For one week, begin noticing the different thoughts, messages, 'gut feels' you have in a day. Once you begin this process you will likely notice a lot of chatter going on in any given day. At some point in the day, jot down ten things you remember noticing. Punctuate them the way you remember them being said and notice the emotional tone of the different messages. Remember that a sense of calm is wisdom and a sense of urgency is critic. The more you do this exercise, the easier it will be to shut out the inner critic and allow your inner wisdom to filter through.

Jane

I finally catch up with Rhonda in the produce section. Her cart is almost empty, so I know she's likely just starting her shopping.

"Rhonda," I call, rolling my cart beside hers. "I'm glad I caught you." I try to smile, but it feels awkward.

Rhonda glances at me, gives a look that clearly says she's not glad I found her, then picks up a green pepper and starts examining it closely.

Go gentle, the voice says, *she doesn't trust you*. Taking a deep breath, I pick up a head of lettuce and pretend to look at it. *Put down the lettuce and talk to her*. I square my shoulders, set down the lettuce and turn halfway towards her.

"I've been wanting to see you ever since the meeting. I feel terrible for how I treated you and for what I said. But I thought you were making fun of Adam and that brought the mother bear out in me. I don't blame you if you hate me for it, but I had to at least tell you that I'm sorry." Rhonda continues to stare at the pepper. She doesn't say anything and I feel the tension creeping up my back.

Taking another deep breath, I blunder on, recognizing that I'm not really saying what Terri and I had decided I should say. "I just wanted to tell you that and hope you can forgive me. And I'm sorry for what happened to Zac." I turn to leave, but another woman is picking out cucumbers and my cart is blocked by hers.

"Jane." Rhonda says in a strained voice. She clears her throat and continues, "You don't know anything about Zac and mother bear or not, you embarrassed me in front of a whole room of people. Do you really think telling me how sorry you are in front of a bunch of produce is going to fix it?" Before I can even register what she has said, Rhonda turns her back to me and nearly flies out of the produce section.

Three people, I want to shout; there were only three people in the room. But before I can say it, I'm filled with a strong sense that this number is not what's important. *She's right.* Gathering my courage I shout after her, "You're right – and I do know about Zac – I'm sorry!" But Rhonda is turning the corner; she is not ready to listen to me anymore.

The cucumber woman is staring at me, along with several other people in the produce section. I take another deep breath, square my shoulders again, paste a fake smile on my face and with head held high, push my cart over to the checkout line. I'm not sure if I'm finished my shopping, but I'm too shaky to continue.

Oh great, says Snarky, but it's the other voice I choose to listen to. *Good start*, it says.

Oh My Goddess! Like Attracts Like

Like attracts like, especially when it comes to feelings. When you feel strong negative feelings while sharing a story you send out vibes that attract matching energy back to you. The same is true if you focus on what you are missing in life, what might go wrong or why things aren't working out.

Notice the kind of questions you ask yourself, what type of things you tend to focus on, as well as the way you feel when you think about or share your stories. Make sure that what you are putting out is aligned with the feelings and situations that you want to bring more of into your world.

The seven day challenge: one way to increase awareness around your speaking habits is to notice when you are sharing relevant information and when you are gossiping or spreading rumours.

> Challenge yourself not to participate in gossip for seven days and see how it changes the energy you attract. Remember that, if you are sitting there imagining the stories you would share if you were allowed to, you will be attracting the same energy as if you were speaking it aloud.

Ego, Meet Your New Boss

A lot of people talk about the ego as if it were something you would be better off without. In fact, the ego is what makes you human, so to get rid of it would not be desirable at all!

A few years ago I heard Sonia Choquette, a gifted intuitive, speaker and author, talk about the ego as if it was your faithful companion – a loyal pet like a dog - to be loved and enjoyed. "You don't go home and kick the dog," I remember her saying, "but you also don't let the dog run the show."

These few words literally changed my understanding of the ego and my ability to keep it in its place.

Your ego is the human side of you. It feels, fears, gets jealous and reacts. Just like a dog, it will bite when threatened or curl up in dread and pee on your shoe. Left in charge, the dog will run the show the way it thinks the show should be ran.

Your ego is in charge when someone says something to you and you feel a need to correct them, explain your behaviour, compete with what they have said or blame someone else. Only the ego will take things personally, become defensive, act overly confident and try to bring others down a notch.

On the other hand, the higher-self is the spiritual side of you; it is the soul. If you believe in this idea, it is the part that is connected to all. The higher-self does not judge, blame, feel or panic. It has access to Divine wisdom although that doesn't mean that it knows all the answers or will always tell you the best way to do things.

I believe that the secret in making this relationship work is to strive to bring the higher-self into the picture as much as you can. At the same time, recognize that your ego is equally important and in desperate need of regular 'pats'.

One way to do this is to ask your higher-self to be in charge and instruct your ego to allow this to happen. When you tell your ego to sit, it will; however, you might have to remind it more than once like a puppy.

As you practice this ability, you'll find your higher-self slipping into the lead role more often and your ego quite happily running by its side. Like the master with a well trained dog, the two make an excellent team and are content when they know their place plus feel loved and appreciated for what they have to offer.

Where Do You Focus Your Energy?

15: Tomorrow's a Flirt, But Today is a Keeper

Living in the present moment is not a new idea, but only recently has it started to create a buzz. Seize the moment . . . the present is the gift . . . the power is in the now . . . Phrases like these are arising everywhere and circling around, taunting, enticing and, sometimes even aggravating us.

Intuitively, you probably know that the power is in the moment. You recognize that, unless a much sought-after time machine is created, the present is the only time period where you can make things happen and yet how often do you forget to put this principle into practice?

I chuckled when reading Randy Gage's status update on Facebook, "You better not wait for tomorrow . . .cause when it gets here, it's going to be today." The concept is so simple and self-explanatory – yet this point is missed all the time.

It's as if we sit on a proverbial bench with a box of melting chocolate in our lap, waiting for tomorrow to arrive:

As soon as I have the money, I'm going to . . .

When I fit these pants, I'll . . .

Once this project is done, I'll be able to . . .

When I retire, I'll get to that . . .

As soon as the divorce is final, I'll take a holiday . . .

I can't wait for tomorrow to get here, so I can have some chocolate . . .

It is impossible for tomorrow to get here!

There is no time like the present. This moment holds all the power. If you accept that gift and strive to make your moments count, you can begin living rather than being a passenger who keeps on missing the train.

As a result, my message to you, me and anyone who's ready to listen: tomorrow isn't coming, but today is here and is completely willing to make something beautiful happen with you.

Taking a Stand:

Recognize that the power is in the moment and put your efforts into making things happen today. That might mean taking a day off, starting a new project, changing jobs, moving out or coming out. There is no prescription for what you need to do, except to make it so. Not tomorrow, not next week, not after the grass is cut. Now.

Jane

"Well, I thought that went very smoothly," Terri says as I sit down across from her with my full cup of tea. "I'm impressed."

The coffee shop is quiet for once. Other than a young couple, both wearing earbuds and texting - presumably to other friends, but maybe to each other - we're the only people here.

"I am so glad I did that!" I exclaim. "It's like a huge weight has been lifted off my shoulders and I can finally breathe again." Raising my arms to the sky, I breathe in deeply, enjoying the warm cinnamon and banana smell of the shop.

"I think you earned the respect of a lot of people tonight. Even though Rhonda didn't say much directly, you could see how much better she felt when she called the meeting to order."

Tonight at the Parent Council meeting, I seized the moment and gave Rhonda a formal apology. I waited until about twelve people were in the room, then stood up and asked for their attention.

I said I had overreacted, made a bunch of assumptions and was embarrassed by my rude behaviour. I told Rhonda I understood if she wasn't ready to forgive me, but I wanted her and everyone to know that my behaviour had been uncalled for, unprofessional and not even based on the truth.

Something about my apology in the store had felt wrong, so I looked up how to give a genuine apology on Youtube and used that video as a guide. I was surprised at how hard it was to take full responsibility for my behaviour. I kept wanting to explain why I had done what I'd done, but according to the video, that weakens what you are saying by suggesting something or someone else was to blame.

"I didn't say exactly what I had planned because I figured it wouldn't sound very sincere if I had to read it. But I thought

I did a good job - if I do say so myself - and I really did mean every word." Goosebumps (or Angel hugs as Terri likes to call them) tingle along my spine and down my arms as I speak.

"Well I thought you sounded confident and sincere. I wasn't kidding when I said I was impressed." Terri raises her mug in a toast. *Lady in Red*," a favorite song from my high school days, comes on the radio in the shop.

I lean over to click my cup to Terri's, then blow on my tea and take a tiny sip. It's lemon and smells delicious, but is still too hot to drink. "You know, I used to be so confident when I was young. Making this formal apology tonight reminded me of that feeling. I forgot what it was like to feel that way rather than plagued with self-doubt and uncertainty."

"What happened to change things for you?" Terri asks, wiping up a little spill of tea off the table with her serviette.

"Grade Ten," I answer without hesitation. "I made a couple of girls mad at me in high school and everything changed. I mean, I was never super popular, but I wasn't unpopular either, until those two turned against me." I try another sip of my tea. It's still too hot.

"It had to do with a boy named Trevor. Apparently, one of these girls liked him and wanted to go to a school dance with him. He asked me and I said yes." A regretful little laugh escapes at the memory. "He was a year older than me, cute and quite popular. I should have known something was 'off', but honestly, I didn't question it at all."

Terri's eyebrows rise, but she says nothing.

"Before I knew it, these girls were spreading lies about me around the school - that I was easy, that I had herpes and that I was bisexual. I tried to deny everything, but the more I denied it the more people teased me about it. And did you know that you can't tell people you're not bi-sexual without sounding homophobic?

Anyway, the worst part was at the dance. Trevor and his friends had brought in some booze and offered me a drink. I was nervous, so I took one sip - it was awful, home brew or something, and it burnt my nose and throat. I coughed and spit it out and they all laughed at me. After that, I said no, but Trevor drank quite a bit and the more he had, the looser he got with his hands.

Trevor told me he had forgotten something in his locker, so we went to get it. The hallways were empty (I don't think we were allowed to go down there) and before I knew it, Trevor was all over me. I shoved him away so hard that in his woozy state, he fell flat on his butt. I ran out of there and called my parents for a ride. Apparently, Trevor stayed and added to the stories about me.

I found out afterward that the only reason he had asked me to the dance was because of a dare and then the rumours convinced him he should make some moves on me. I suffered through the rest of the school year with people whispering behind my back and writing graffiti about me.

My parents transferred me for my last two years of school, but I never felt the same. My confidence was shot. Even when I met Tom, I still kept waiting for the other shoe to fall. Really, it's only in these last couple months with you that I'm starting to feel good about myself again."

My throat feels tight all of a sudden and my eyes are getting watery. I haven't shared this story with anyone but Tom and I feel super-exposed at the moment.

Terri smiles gently. "You were very courageous, both when this happened and just now, in sharing it with me. Kids can be so mean - but then I guess adults can too. Do you want to know one of the most amazing things I learned when I went for counselling after I left my husband?"

I nod and sip my tea. The lemon is delicious and it's perfect drinking temperature.

Terri crosses her legs and leans back in her chair. "Confidence never leaves you. It just gets covered up with negative stories, beliefs and thoughts you have about yourself."

My mouth opens to argue, but Terri holds up her hand and laughs. "I know," she continues, "I wanted to argue about it too, but the reality is we are all born resilient and confident - that never goes away. If you think about it, that's why when people heal from a horrific experience, they'll say things like, *I just made up my mind to change things and I never looked back.* They didn't have to learn how to be confident - they just had to uncover it. Being aware of the BIG 5, your inner critic and limiting beliefs doesn't hurt either.

Now, of course, there are skills that will help match your confidence to your ability, but the confidence or the resiliency - knowing you can handle whatever life throws your way - is always there."

Deep in my belly, I can feel a connection with what Terri is saying. Even though I don't fully understand it yet, I know what she's saying is true. With that realization comes a wonderful feeling of inner strength and ability.

Oh My Goddess! One Moment Please

Living in the moment is about being present for whatever you are doing. There is no room in this moment for regretting the past, worrying about the future or scrolling through your never-ending tasks. The more you practice living in the moment, the easier it becomes. It can be hard to stay in the present for long periods of time, so here are some ideas that take only a moment:

- 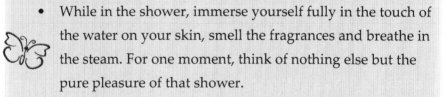 While in the shower, immerse yourself fully in the touch of the water on your skin, smell the fragrances and breathe in the steam. For one moment, think of nothing else but the pure pleasure of that shower.

- Sitting down with a fresh mug of coffee or tea, empty your mind and feel the warmth of the mug in your hand. Breathe in the aroma, close your eyes and savour the taste.

- Go for a walk in nature and take a moment to listen to the crunch of your footsteps. Take your shoes off and feel the ground beneath your feet. Notice the sun, rain or wind on your exposed skin. Listen for the many layers of sound. Breathe in deeply and feel your breath go all the way down to your toes.

- Make chore time your time! Let go of all the lists running through your head, any resentment that you have to do the cleaning or any worries about the future. Play some music, put on your jingly skirt or whatever gets you moving and immerse yourself in the pleasure of the moment.

- For tasks you really dislike, set a timer to focus only on that task for 15 minutes or whatever amount of time seems right to you. Then allow yourself 5 minutes to stretch, go outside, enjoy a beverage or read a chapter in this book. In other words, you are giving the task your full focus and then getting pleasure from the time off guilt-free.

16: Fill'er Up! How Self-Care Can Keep You Going

Women are often being asked to give a piece of themselves to others. It might be to their kids, their spouse, their school, church or community. A natural part of the Divine Feminine is nurturance, so it makes sense that people will be drawn to women for things.

The problem arises when you give so much of yourself and do not take the time required to replenish your resources. This behaviour pattern is a recipe for disaster because not only does it leave you drained - burnt out, exhausted, or ill - but it also means that you are role modelling a martyr type of lifestyle to your loved ones.

You would never suggest that a person keep on driving when her gas tank is empty because the car will not go. You likely insist that others take time to rest, recharge and perhaps be spoiled a little. Yet how often do you overlook this requirement for yourself?

It is time to change this pattern!

One of the simplest ways to help people become better at looking after themselves is to have them take stock of what fills them up. Like a car at the gas station, you need regular fills of positive moments in your life if you want to be able to keep trucking day after day.

You know something fills you up if:

- You enjoy doing it.
- You feel stronger after doing it.
- You feel good about yourself as a person for doing it.
- You feel a sense of happiness or contentment deep within when you do it.

Examples of things that might fill you up:

- Connection to others - quality time with partner, kids, family, friends, volunteering and service to others. It's important that you feel allowed to be your true self with these people.
- Movement/exercise - dancing, swinging, yoga, running, aerobics, sex, biking, massages, swimming
- Music - singing, drumming, listening to music, playing an instrument

- Touch/energy work - massages, foot rubs, pranic healing, reiki
- Quieting the mind - relaxing baths, meditation, daydreaming, tai chi, qi gong, yoga
- Belly laughs – with a friend, a child, watching a show
- Artistic expression – writing, drawing, painting, sculpting, pottery, crafting, baking
- Releasing Chi - cleaning out a closet, organizing a drawer, giving away clothing
- Being out in nature – walking, tree hugging, sitting by water, horseback riding, walking barefoot in the sand
- Animals – petting a dog, grooming an animal, playing with a kitten, watching fish in a tank
- Excitement – Riding a motorcycle, flying an airplane, driving a race car

The type of things that fulfills this need, how much you need to reach the full mark and the amount of time you remain "full" are different for everyone. Take some time and explore a little. Once you find something that satisfies you, be sure to build it into your life so you can fill up on a regular basis and never risk the chance of running on empty.

Taking a Stand:

Create a list of the activities that you feel stronger after doing. Rate them on a scale from one to five - with five being fantastic - and look specifically at the fives. Notice how often you currently fit these things into your life and make a plan for how you can bring in at least one a month. Then sprinkle in some of the lower numbers until you feel like you have a nice mix with at least one thing happening every day. Decide how you can put this plan into action and share it with another person. Your life partner really stands to benefit from this self-care project, so release any guilt you might be piling on yourself and let him or her know what you are doing and why.

Jane

Pulling into the garage, I turn off the car and lean my head on the headrest. After sharing my story with Terri, I felt exhausted, but happy; it was as if this story that I had carried around all these years, blocking my self-confidence had lost its hold on me and floated away.

We celebrated by sharing a huge piece of fresh, warm-from-the-oven banana loaf. It was awesome. While we ate, Terri told me about her life and how she had grown up in a family that didn't care whether she lived or died.

Her father was a long-haul trucker, so he was away a lot, thank goodness. When he was home, he'd use both her and her mother as punching bags. I felt sick just thinking about it; I wondered why her mother didn't do anything to protect her. Terri said that, between bouts of depression and alcoholism, the only thing her mother did was teach her how to tippytoe around when Daddy was home and insist that his outbursts were never his fault.

Her mom's only friend lived next door and was also in an abusive relationship. Terri fell asleep to the sounds of abuse in either her home or through the thin walls of the place next door. She grew up believing that it was perfectly normal for men to hit women out of anger.

Terri met her first and only boyfriend on the Sunday she turned nineteen at church, which her mom made her attend regularly to pray for forgiveness for being so hard on her dad! Less than a year later, Terri was married.

"He didn't beat me at first," Terri said, "so I thought I had finally figured out how to make a man happy. Then one day he came home from work and I could see he was mad about something. I pretended I didn't notice as I had been trained to do and hurried supper to the table. I had made tuna casserole with peas in it. Turns out he hated peas and that was the straw that broke the camel's back, or in this case, my left wrist."

I asked Terri how she ever got up the nerve to leave her husband. She said it was when she gave birth to her daughter Sam. She had been married for six years - Nolan was five - and she had suffered through three miscarriages.

When Sam was born, she suddenly realized that her daughter was likely to live the same sort of life that she was enduring unless she made some tough decisions.

"My mom had drilled into my head that doctors and police would put me in jail for being a bad daughter if I told them what was going on, so I kept quiet." Terri actually laughed when she said this. I could see this story was no longer a part of who she was.

"I believed my mom, even though deep down, I felt that couldn't be right. I'd seen enough bad things happen that I didn't want to chance it.

I'd go to the hospital for injuries inflicted by my father or husband and make up a perfectly reasonable lie about what had happened. When I was young, I could see questions in their eyes, but they'd patch me up and send me home every time. It was like they didn't want to deal with the truth.

When Sam was born, everything changed. I had a young nurse helping me when I was in labour and she saw the scars, the size of my file and perhaps even the fear in my eyes. She told me about a friend of hers who had similar scars. The nurse was very subtle. She said her friend's scars were from putting up with an abusive husband.

She sounded so outraged and sad because her friend believed that's what relationships were supposed to be like. For the first time I started to question what I had been taught. She told me that mostly she was terrified for her friend's baby daughter, who would likely grow up living that same cycle of abuse.

I didn't know I was having a girl yet, but the moment she was born, my eyes locked with the nurse and I knew the story was about me. She came back to bring me Sam for a feeding a couple of hours later and I told her everything. She set me up with a shelter and had the police come to take a statement. Child and Family picked up Nolan from my mother's house and I never looked back." Terri's eyes looked far away, almost like she was describing a movie to me.

Sitting alone in my car, I wipe the tears off my cheeks. Although Terri's story was terrible to hear, I could tell she wasn't sharing it with me for sympathy. Her story was actually one of strength, resiliency and the courage to take ownership of her situation. Her positive outlook on life and the way she has turned things around for her kids and herself moved me deeply. In some strange yet wonderful way, her achievements added to the feeling of power that was slowly building within me.

Oh My Goddess! Playing with Compassion

Compassion is a beautiful offshoot of unconditional love and would fill up all of us if we allowed it to flow. Put your hand on your heart or where you think your heart is and feel it expand with love, peace and gratitude. Keep filling it until you can actually feel energy pulsating in your hand. Envision it pouring out of you and into the space around you. If you like, have it keep expanding out, filling the room, embracing any people who come to mind and maybe even some whom you don't know. Let the energy keep expanding - out of your yard, around your neighborhood, embracing the whole city . . . country . . . continent - until finally the whole world is surrounded in love.

> The more you practice this exercise, the quicker you'll find that compassion rises to the surface when dealing with others and that is of benefit to all.

Having a Sweet Body

Recently I saw a poster of different kinds of fruit, each one lamenting its shortcomings.

"I'm too short," says the strawberry.

"I'm so hairy," states the kiwi.

"Why am I so big?" asks the watermelon.

"I hate my skin colour," exclaims the orange.

"Why am I so wide?" questions the pear.

There were many other kinds of fruit on the poster, all complaining about the very thing that makes them special. As soon as I saw the poster, I knew I had to talk about it in this book. It truly saddens me that women have been taught to dislike the package they come in.

Even girls whose bodies haven't finished maturing will complain of being too fat or needing to diet. Parents are forewarned about childhood obesity; they are told that kids are not active enough and that we should all be alarmed.

There are plenty of problems with the processing of food and how we are nurturing our bodies, but the biggest problem of all, I believe, is the attitude we have created towards the female body. Of course, this is not exclusive to women anymore although I don't think that's reason to celebrate either.

Your body is your temple. It allows you to exist in human form; it is something to be valued and appreciated no matter how it looks. This information doesn't mean it's bad to strive for better health or to do exercises that burn off fat and build up your muscles.

It just means that, no matter what your body looks like, it deserves to be loved. The caption on the poster I mentioned earlier said, "If only they knew, they had such sweet bodies."

I would like to extend this caption from the poster out to every woman on the planet – you have a sweet body - and help her to really believe it!

Putting It All Together

17: Loving Your Life

As we come to the end of this book, I want to applaud you on your desire to keep pushing forward. Personal growth can feel challenging, uncomfortable and unfair at times.

It is easy to become downhearted and spend more time in regret rather than looking forward. Especially if you believe you are being punished for mistakes you have made or opportunities you have missed.

Let me assure you that your journey is never about punishment or getting even. Life is always about growth, creativity and expansion. Growing rarely happens unless you are challenged to take a leap. Your path may be bumpy and twisty with lots of forks in the road. Sometimes it may seem all uphill, at other times it may seem as if you are dropping into a bottomless pit.

Your journey is yours - you cannot do it wrong! You can, however, make it harder and less enjoyable than it needs to be. Everything that happens in your life is meant to help you on your way. Your biggest choice will be to decide how you are going to feel about that trip.

Living life on purpose is about noticing what you are doing rather than staying on auto-pilot and simply drifting through the days. It's easy to fall into the role of victim, hold grudges and pour energy into regrets when you are drifting through life. It's as if life is happening to you - rather than the other way around.

Perhaps now is a good time to take full responsibility for the life you are living, if you haven't done so already. Notice where you are going, take time to enjoy the little things, refuse to see bumps in the road as personal failures and make a point of living your life fully awake.

Taking A Stand:

Create a list of all the major experiences you have had in your life, such as: having kids, getting married, painful breakups, embarrassing moments, promotions or scholarships, fights with friends, great times with your family, bullying incidences, graduations as well as accidents. Write down any noteworthy experiences that come to mind. Beside each event, write the year it occurred beside them (as well as you can remember).

On a long piece of paper, start on the far left side and put a dot in the middle of the paper (from top to bottom). Write the date you were born beside the dot.

Plot the items from your list along the page in order of date. Put things that seemed positive when they happened above the line and those that felt negative below. Leave room for other things you might remember later.

Highlight or star those things from which you really learned a lot, that made you who you are today or that you wouldn't trade for the world.

Connect the dots and see what your journey has looked like so far.

This page represents your life journey. Notice the twists and turns, ups and downs and especially what pieces have helped you become the person you are today. The hills, valleys, and unexpected turns are what make your journey remarkable. They are the very essence of what makes life an adventure.

Jane

Looking at myself in the mirror, I turn sideways and stick out my belly. I look about five months pregnant when I stick it out like that. I rub my tummy and send love to it like I would if a baby was in there.

A part of my brain is trying to scream that I need to diet, that this extra cushion on my belly is nothing to be proud of and I'd better get exercising before nothing in my closet fits. I shut out those messages and continue sending my belly love. "My body is my temple," I whisper, "and my belly is its foundation of strength."

"Is there something I should know?" I jump at Tom's voice and drop my hands in embarrassment.

"No," I respond curtly, "I'm just wishing my fat away." Anger surges through me for caving so quickly on my self-love. "What are you doing home so early?"

Tom is behind me in a flash and puts his hands on my belly just like I had been doing. "Don't wish any part of you away," he says, kissing my neck. "I love every one of your curves, always have and always will."

His words touch me deeply and I turn to him. "Do you really mean that?" I ask. "I mean, secretly wouldn't you like me to lose some weight?"

"Listen," he says, putting his hands on my shoulders and holding me in place." We are not having this conversation because you will overanalyze, read way too deeply into it and, if you see fit, crucify me in the end no matter what I say or don't say." I give a half smile, recognizing the truth in what he is saying.

"So listen carefully because this is a statement and not open for discussion. As I have tried to tell you many times before, I love you - your skin, your hair, your curves, your smell - all of you. While I'd never intentionally change you, I would also never stand in the way of you changing yourself if that's what you need to do. Just don't do it for me."

My ego wants to argue or question at least half of what he's said, but I tell it to sit and request that my higher-self be in charge.

"How did I get so lucky?" I ask and pull his head down for a heartfelt kiss.

Oh My Goddess! Body...Can I Have An Apple?

Your body is made up of energy just like everything else in the universe, and as a result will speak to you if you ask it to. I don't mean that your body actually talks with a voice; I just mean that it will answer questions about what you should eat, drink, and take including vitamins, herbs or over-the-counter medications. With practice this channel of information can do much more than that. This kind of questioning can also be done with a pendulum - any light object swinging from a thin string - if asking your body seems too obscure.

Standing with your feet comfortably together (a little less than shoulder width apart), look forward and pick up a vitamin bottle, drink, piece of fruit or a hamburger - whatever you want to ask your body about. Hold it loosely in front of you. If you feel pulled forward, towards the item, your body is saying that item would be beneficial to you right now. If you feel pushed back, your body is saying that it does not want that item. If what you're holding makes your body go sideways, I believe it's telling you that it won't benefit or harm you.

As you play with this exercise, you'll discover that once you and your body are conversing comfortably, you can ask it any simple yes or no questions rather than limiting it to actual items. To do this, stand with your hands clasped loosely in front of you and ask your body to "show me a yes." If it responds, ask it to "show me a no," and see what happens. Once the yes and no are established ask it whatever question you want to investigate. In time, you may find that your inner wisdom responds along with the yes or the no, providing some very interesting insights into things you wouldn't normally know.

18: Releasing the Pressure

Stress provides you with an opportunity to expand, but like an elastic, too much stress can cause you to break.

It is important to understand that regardless of what is challenging you in life, you create the bulk of your stress. This statement can be hard to accept, but it is absolutely true. The way you think feeds your stress; for this reason, become aware of what you are thinking and see what you can do to change it.

Tip #1: Stop comparing

As mentioned at the beginning of this book, comparison becomes a waste of time, when you understand that everyone's journey is unique. Add to that the realization that most of us aren't even aware of our true journey until it is near completion and comparison reveals itself as an unnecessary stress producer.

Anytime you compare yourself to someone else, it adds stress to your life. Even when you decide that you compare favorably to others, you add stress because you do not want to drop in your standings if you are currently 'ahead'.

> **You can't help but win at your journey -- you are the ONLY one on it!**

I am not suggesting that you shouldn't try to do well, or be motivated to make changes. I am saying that when you compare yourself in incomparable situations, you increase stress and get nothing in return.

Tip #2: Practice being neutral

I mentioned already that events are neutral. This idea is worth repeating because we bring a lot of stress into our lives when we decide something is good or bad.

There is an old Chinese parable about a poor farmer whose prize horse runs away and then returns with a pack of wild horses. His only son breaks his hip while taming one of the horses, and as a result, is not drafted into the army when it comes recruiting new members. As each situation arises in the story, the neighbours try to assign it meaning, "Oh, this is awful. Oh this is wonderful!" The farmer remains uncommitted.

"Maybe good, maybe bad," is his standard response and every time what the neighbours have labeled good or bad turns out to be the opposite. This problem is easy to identify in a short proverb, but in real life we assign meaning as if it is absolute fact. Interestingly enough, the meaning we assign is usually based on the emotions that a situation initially brings to the surface.

Learning to recognize these feelings as signals rather than 'meaning justifiers' can save you from a lot of stress and allow you to be much more controlled in any situation.

Tricks to help you remain neutral when faced with stressful situations:

- Develop a list of simple coping statements and post them where you can see them. For example, I'll be okay, Stay Calm, Everything will work out, I can do this. Notice your body cues and make sure they are responding to your calming messages.

- Ask yourself, *how significant will this be two years from now*? Search for an honest answer.

- Imagine sharing the story of what's happening with a group of friends. Think about what part in the story would make them laugh and play it up.

- Pretend you are another person in the room, watching the interaction. Use that person's objective position to see things from all sides. Sometimes, looking at things from another perspective is all you need to recognize that your feelings are making things worse than they need to be.

- Adopt a standard response of "Maybe good, maybe bad," and believe it!

Tip #3: Pay attention to the little things

A lot of stress is created by little things that most people do all of the time. Becoming self-aware is the first step towards making any significant changes in your life. Notice the little things you do that add to your stress and do what you can to decrease them.

- Pay attention to negative self-talk and refuse to feed it.

- Notice tension in your body and do stretches or exercises to work it out.

- Practice detaching your ego from situations, so you are not taking things personally.

- Learn relaxation techniques for both mind and body.

- Use laughter to reduce stress - even if it starts out forced. Laughter is a wonderful way to release the tension that arises from stress. When you have a real belly laugh, you are releasing emotions pent up inside of you.

- Learn your triggers and protect your buttons from being pushed.

- Pay attention to what you eat, how much sleep you are getting, how much exercise and how much fresh air you get.

Tip #4: Reduce environmental stresses

Toxins, food additives, negativity and 'victim thinking' are just some of the environmental stresses you likely experience regularly. Noticing where these things come into your life and making a conscious effort to remove them can help you reduce unnecessary stress.

For example, listening to upsetting news can have a huge negative impact on your life. Fear always adds to stress and media tends to be fear-focused. If you can't stop listening to the news, learn techniques to avoid buying into the negativity. You will actually be helping to remove some of the negativity from the world if you can receive disheartening news while filled with love and compassion for those involved (rather than sadness, anger, revulsion, sympathy or fear).

You will find that stress builds constantly if you're spending all day stuck in a negative work environment or with negative people. Do what you can to protect yourself from this type of environment and combine it with Tip #5.

Tip #5 Surround yourself with people who give back to you

We are all social creatures; women especially require the support of others. Focus on building strong relationships, ask for help, find people you can talk to and like being around. Sever relationships that make you feel drained or set clear boundaries to plug the hole. Good relationships double your joy and halve your problems, so make sure yours are doing those things for you.

Tip #6 Practice prioritizing, delegating and saying no

Divide up your work load into categories and then focus your energy on those things that must get done and/or bring you joy. Sample categories:

Things that must get done – Things are on this list because you really believe that not to do them would result in consequences with which you absolutely could not live. If this list is really huge, chances are you have taken on a martyr attitude which will only add to your stress. Be honest about what must be in this category and then prioritize the things YOU must do; delegate where possible; say no when not essential; always remember that done is better than perfect.

Things that should get done - Try not to 'should' on yourself if possible. Often these things are on your list only because you believe other people will judge you harshly if you don't do them. Try to let them go unless they are something you enjoy.

<u>Things you enjoy doing</u> – The things you enjoy doing fill you up and are a very important part of daily life. Make sure some of these are on your 'must do' list and make time for them to happen.

<u>Things I wouldn't mind getting done . . .one day</u> - These ideas can be kept, but do not need priority placement, nor need they cause any guilt when they are not getting done. They are great to save for those 'rainy day' activities.

<u>Things that I have no idea why I'm doing, but they sure take up a lot of my time</u> - Examples might be reading flyers, watching shows you don't even like or dusting the tops of door frames. Eliminate these energy-wasters and enjoy the time they free up!

These suggestions are just a few of the things you can do to take some of the pressure off and make stress something that stretches you without having it damage you. It is easy to get caught up in the hyper style of living that our society seems to promote.

Recognize that stress is a normal and necessary part of life, but it was never meant to disconnect you from the bigger picture and the journey you are on. To put it simply, you can choose to be the one in the driver's seat of your life. Since it's your adventure, I think that's a great place for you to be.

Taking A Stand:

Assign a number on a scale of one to ten to each of the tips above (with ten being 'very stressful in your life'). Start with the one you rate the highest and make a point of initiating changes in your daily life to decrease the stress in that area. When you notice a positive difference in that area, move on to the next highest number. Expect fluctuations and slip-ups as they are part of what makes you human.

Jane

Dropping my toothbrush back into its holder, I spit my final rinse into the sink. The kids are asleep and Tom's in bed, reading a book.

I slip in next to him and pick up my novel. Something falls off the top of my book and onto the floor. It's a Hershey's Chocolate Hug and a little piece of paper. I look at Tom inquiringly, but he keeps reading although the edge of a smile is tugging at his lip. Getting back out of bed, I pick up the paper.

"*I love you sexy mama and here's a hug to prove it*" is written in Tom's distinctive scrawl.

"What's this?" I ask with a laugh, setting the chocolate hug on the nightstand and holding out the note.

"Just a little token of my affection for you," Tom says, smiling and watching me carefully. "Aren't you going to eat it?" he asks, pointing at the hug.

"I just brushed my teeth," I answer, wondering if my answer will hurt his feelings. "What's going on?"

Tom shrugs. "Okay, it doesn't matter when you eat it, and nothing is going on. I do love you very much and think you're every bit as sexy today as the day we met."

I feel my skin flush and warmth fills me from head to toe. I crawl back into bed and snuggle up beside him, "That's so sweet," I say, "I love you too."

"I think you're an Auditory," Tom says, "and definitely a Digital because you always want us to connect."

"What are you talking about?" I demand, moving away . . . suspicious again.

"Well, for the last few months, you've been doing all this stuff with Terri and it's changing you as a person. It dawned on me that maybe I could do an upgrade or two myself." Tom holds up his hand as if to stave off an attack. "I'm not suggesting you needed upgrades - I'm just saying you've been putting in a real effort to grow as a person and have inspired me to do the same."

I raise my eyebrows in wonder. Everything I've read in the personal development field has suggested that the best way to change others is to change myself first, but I hadn't really believed it or expected it to be so obvious. Besides, Tom was already pretty fantastic in my book; it was me who was all messed up. Still, there's room for everybody to upgrade and I certainly don't want to discourage him from that.

"So before my flight earlier this month, I went in the store and picked up a couple of books - Stephen Covey's *7 Habits of Highly Effective Families* (that's a long one - I'm only up to the second habit, but I'm learning a lot) and John Gray's *Men Are From Mars, Women are From Venus*."

"Waiting for the meeting to start last week, I made a joke about learning to speak Venusian and my buddy, Dave, knew exactly what I was talking about. He brought this book on Love Languages by Gary Chapman to the next meeting. Said his ex-wife gave it to him along with the divorce papers, so it didn't help him, but he thought it might be a good read for me."

"That's the one I'm reading now, which is why I was trying to figure out what your love languages are without asking you." Tom gives me a shy smile and his cheeks look a little crimson.

"You have no idea how loved that makes me feel." My voice sounds like I'm joking, but I mean every word.

"You're obviously not a Visual," Tom continues, "or my little chocolate hug wouldn't be sitting rejected on your nightstand." He laughs and grabs my hand to stop me from reaching for the candy. "Plus, if you were Visual, you would likely save the note rather than roll it up in your fingers." He gestures at the note I've rolled into a little tube. I straighten it out quickly and try to smooth it on the bed.

"I figure you're an Auditory, just like Gray suggested. Of course, I always thought you could be from Venus." This comes out with a corny grin that no woman in her right mind would fall for.

Laughing, I give him a playful punch on the shoulder. "Well, perhaps I should read those books as well." I am still very touched that my big, tough husband would do this. "If I have to live with a Martian, I might as well learn how to make him happy."

Tom grabs me by the waist and pulls me back down on the bed beside him. Talking in a goofy Martian voice, he says, "Martians are very easy to please, Venus lady. We like seeing and touching."

Oh My Goddess! Appreciating Differences

There is a lot of information available that can help you better understand people. We are not all the same, yet we often assume that we are. When we make an assumption like this, we limit our ability to truly accept each other and perhaps even to celebrate the 'spice' that life has to offer.

You might want to investigate some of these areas further if you haven't already. You can be as general or specific as you like - it's all fun and enlightening.

One gentle reminder: people change and grow all the time. While some traits will always stay with them it is not up to us to lock anybody into something forever. Investigate, enjoy and be enlightened, but do it with an open mind, allowing others to change and grow in any way they would like.

> Suggestions for areas to research:
>
> | | |
> |---|---|
> | Personalities | Understanding men vs women |
> | Communication modes | Learning Styles |
> | Love languages | Body types |
> | Astrological signs | Meta-programs |
> | Iridology (reading the eyes) | Handwriting analysis |
> | Palmistry | Blood typing |
>
> Brain dominance (right brain, left brain)

A Life of Learning

The more you learn about why you do things and what causes certain feelings to arise in your life, the easier it is to make changes and continue moving forward. Personal growth is an ongoing process that does not cease until you do. It's a great idea to keep your eyes and ears open to information that will help you see things in a positive light and truly embrace the life you are experiencing.

In line with this thinking, my book would not be complete unless I shared why learning something new can be a very uncomfortable process.

The Learning Cycle

The learning cycle is a predictable pattern that each of us follows when learning something new. Knowing about this cycle can help you recognize why you feel uncomfortable when starting a new project. This pattern is in effect whether you are entering a new relationship, starting a new job, learning to play a new sport, becoming a parent for the third time or any other new thing you might be trying. People will move through the phases at a different rate, but everyone will experience this cycle.

If you are caught unaware of this pattern, it becomes easy to misinterpret what you are feeling and veer off at a time when moving forward would be your best course of action. Once you are aware, however, you can use this knowledge to help move you quickly through the process and make learning new things much less uncomfortable.

Phase 1: Awkward/Uncomfortable – In this phase, you are learning all the pieces involved in using a new tool, doing a job or uncovering a talent. It feels awkward because you really have to think about the skill in order to use it. This phase can pass very quickly, depending on the response you get from others and how easily you adapt to the task.

Phase 2: Fraudulent/Phony – This phase occurs after you've practiced the new learning enough to recognize that it's getting easier to do. The reason you feel fraudulent is that you know that you are still feeling shaky and could mess it up at any moment although your performance makes it look like you are good at the task. In this phase, it is common to think that if other people could hear your brain chatter, they would expose you for the phony that you really are.

Phase 3: Authentic/Comfortable – This is the phase where you have allowed yourself to make the task your own, and as a result, are feeling more comfortable with it. You might have adapted the tool to fit you better (often unconsciously) or changed your own approach to better fit the tool. You feel confident and competent at what you are doing.

Phase 4: Automatic/Easy – At this point, the learning has become so perfectly integrated that you do not need to think about it at all. It's easy and you feel as if you could do it in your sleep. This part of your life requires little if any thought at all.

Once you are aware of this cycle, you can use it to remove some of the stress from the learning process. You know a new skill is going to be awkward for the first while, so prepare yourself to feel that way. This strategy can help you stamp out your inner critic or the BIG 5 patterns of self-destruction that love to appear anytime you feel awkward.

The same is true for the fraudulent phase. You can remind yourself that you have moved into phase two and accept the phony feeling as confirmation of that move rather than feel nervous that someone is going to call your bluff, thus allowing that feeling to cause self-doubt.

The more accepting and positive you are during those first two phases, the faster you will move into the authentic stage. You may have been told that whatever you are learning must be done a certain way to work properly. While it's easy to understand why your instructor would utter these words, you must accept that taking ownership and changing the process to fit you is the main way to move out of the fraudulent area and into the authentic.

The first two phases provide you with the opportunity to learn the system exactly as the originator intended it. In order to move to the next phase, however, it's time to allow your confidence and creativity to flow. Start making little adjustments to how you do things, not for the sake of changing them, but to make you and the skill fit together perfectly. Take some calculated risks and allow your intuition to guide you.

In time, you will get to the automatic phase. The challenge with this stage is that, if you are not careful, you can become bored and create drama. You do not grow when you are on autopilot, so while your ability is now serving you effortlessly, problems will arise if you do not start a challenging new adventure somewhere in your life.

Recognizing how you learn, along with why certain feelings arise and where you might be 'feeding the fire', provides a starting place for standing in your power. You will experience awkward moments and likely even situations when you allow patterns of self destruction - self-doubt, uncertainty, worry, guilt and fear - to slow you down. This is not failure, this is life.

The more aware you become about what makes you tick, what you can control, as well as what you cannot, the more you can live your life fully awake.

Jane

Drifting off to sleep and listening to Tom's gentle snore beside me, I begin my gratitude list. I can't believe how wonderful life feels right now and how much I appreciate all the things that I am learning.

I know that there are still going to be trying times ahead - that's what helps me grow after all - but for the first time in a very long while, learning excites me rather than fills me with fear. Now that I'm more connected with my inner wisdom and less tuned in to my inner critic, I find I'm ready to be creative, not take results so personally and to push myself out of my comfort zone.

In fact, later this month we'll be electing our parent council for next year and, I'm not positive yet, but I think I might let my name stand for the Chair position.

Oh My Goddess! Grow with the Flow

There may be times in your life when growth seems to come in every area of your life at the same time. This surprising experience is similar to canoeing downstream and suddenly finding yourself faced with a number of rapids at the same moment as you see a grizzly bear wading into the stream just beyond the froth.

When an accelerated growth spurt such as this occurs, I suggest you let go of your preconceived ideas of what needs to happen and 'grow' with the flow as best you can.

People often make their life more difficult than it needs to be by deciding in advance what the outcome should be and how they should reach that outcome. This kind of rigid thinking can make you dig in your paddle at a spot where it will flip your canoe or cause your boat to broadside a rock – or worse yet hit the bear.

Rarely will you know the best route to get to your desired outcome. In fact, sometimes it's the outcome itself that is off kilter, but we need not worry about that if we allow things to 'grow' with the flow. You fight the current of the river by holding on to an idea of what you think things should look like. Going with the flow, means letting go and allowing that current to take you downstream - effortlessly. 'Growing' with the flow means allowing yourself to grow without stipulating how it will happen or exactly what the final outcome will look like.

The universe is constantly shifting, adjusting and challenging us. It will look after how things get done and may even surprise you with the actual outcome if you trust it.

In other words, set your goals, intentions and dreams. Just don't lock yourself into winning the lottery to make these things happen or to working at a certain company as confirmation that you 'made it'. Your journey is unique and has never been traveled before. Open yourself up to the adventure and focus your energy on finding ways to enjoy the ride.

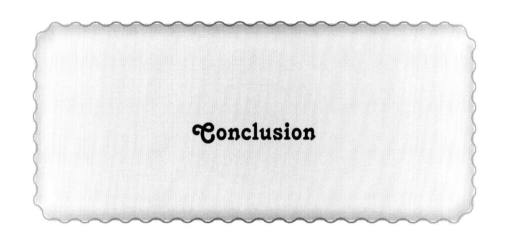

Conclusion

Embracing Your Journey

Every one of us is on a unique and special journey. If you do not know what yours is, that's okay. If you really want to know what yours is and are willing to do the work to figure it out, that's okay. If you disagree with the idea that you are here on a journey, that's okay.

What's unacceptable is to ignore the fact that the decision is yours alone to make no matter what you decide. Standing in your power is about knowing where you end and others begin. It entails uncovering your confidence and, if necessary, reopening the door to hear your intuition. It is also connected to reawakening the Divine Feminine within you and remembering that this lovely energy makes up a full half of a balanced whole.

Take the pieces from this book that really resonate with you. Allow your energy to draw other like-minded people towards you, help you embrace who you are and reach out to other people. Women are strengthened when they open themselves up to collaboration, compassion and connection.

You do not need to do anything that you are not ready to do. All I ask is that you stay open to the idea, to the information shared and begin to notice how, where and when it surfaces in your life. If it doesn't arise after a while, your memory of it will fade - no harm, no foul. In most cases, however, an opportunity will appear. When it does, it will suddenly feel like the perfect thing for you to do.

There are plenty of people waiting to help you heal, guide you through unfamiliar territory and empower you to embrace what you have to offer. All you need to do is be open to new possibilities.

Until we meet again, Namaste - the light within me salutes the light within you. It urges you to stand in your power however you may want that to look!

Jane's Epilogue

"I got it," I say and pick up the ringing phone. It's 7:30 a.m. on a Tuesday morning - early for a call. It would have sent the 'old Jane' into a spin.

"Hi Jane. I just wanted to remind you I will be picking the kids up ten minutes early today," Rhonda says, "I'm so excited about the boy's self defense class - I hope they love it!"

"No problem," I respond, looking at the kitchen table where my three kids sit eating breakfast, "It's a program that allows them to yell, kick and push - how could they not?"

Scanning the table I zero in on Adam's backpack that we got ready the night before with everything he'd need for his new program today. We have a nice morning routine now with everyone sharing in the responsibilities and some things looked after the night before, so getting out the door on time is rarely a problem.

"Right!" Rhonda exclaims with a giggle. "Oh and don't forget - Terri and I will be picking you up just before four today for our spa time. I am so overdue for a pedicure and you are so going to kick butt at your interview tomorrow. I'm so excited for you!"

Her little ramble comes out like a musical riff, making her sound more like a teenager than a forty something woman. Chuckling, I thank her for the kind words, assure her that I haven't forgotten and hang up the phone.

It's still hard for me to believe how much my life has changed in the last two years. Not only have I been personally asked by my boss to apply for a big promotion at work, but every piece of my life has changed in a wonderful way.

I'm healthier, happier and way more confident than I've ever been in my life. Rhonda and Terri have become my two closest friends and my relationship with Tom is fantastic.

Of course, I still overreact at times, my kids don't always get along and on an off day, I might stress about money, homework or the laundry, but overall, life is great.

Sipping my Yerba Maté, I look up as Tom walks in the kitchen, smelling like soap and shaving cream and looking handsome in his travel suit. "Alright," he says, walking over. He plants a lingering kiss full on my lips.

"I'm off. Knock 'em dead tomorrow, kiddo," he says and pulls me into a hug. "I'd wish you luck, but you've got something way better." Winking at me, he walks towards the kids.

Nine year old Amy launches from the table into his bear hug, Adam is right behind. "You guys be good," Tom reminds them, ruffling Adam's hair and leaning across the table to give Jordan a kiss.

"Don't forget you're in charge of childcare after school today, so your mom can get all gussied up," he reminds her, "and when I'm back the day after tomorrow, we'll all go out for a fancy supper to celebrate your mom's big promotion."

"But what if she doesn't get the promotion," asks Adam, always practical when it comes to food.

"Well, I wouldn't worry about that - they'd be crazy not to give her the job. But if they are crazy, then we'll go out and celebrate anyway because we wouldn't want your mom stuck working for a bunch of crazy people."

We all laugh at his comment, causing Tippet to bark, which makes us laugh even harder.

My heart swells with gratitude for Tom, my kids, the dog, my job, my friends and mostly for me - a woman who now clearly realizes that standing in her power doesn't mean she has to have all the answers. It doesn't even mean that she always has to be graceful or upbeat.

Standing in her power simply means that, no matter what life throws her way, she will confidently accept the challenge as part of her journey and know that she alone is fully equipped to handle it.

Acknowledgments

Writing a book is a big process and there are many people who must be acknowledged.

To my life coach, Deb Dawson-Dunn, thanks for helping me to stand in my power even when I really didn't want to. Without you it's quite possible this book never would have made it through to completion.

To Lynne Klippel, a fellow writer, teacher and lover of good books. Thank you for helping me dream up the idea to include Jane's story in this book. It made writing and watching it gel together so much more fun. You are a gift to the writing community and I am so thankful our paths have crossed.

To Bev Sandell Greenberg, my editor. Your skill, professionalism and patience is outstanding and much appreciated. I expect you are shuddering while reading this section that did not go through edit. I hope you can see beyond my grammatical challenges and feel the heart-felt thank you that is intended.

To my long-time pal and graphic design artist, Teresa. You are a fantastic friend, teacher and fellow explorer. This book literally would not be the same without your involvement. Thank you for filling me up on so many occasions and continuing to be my friend through thick and thin. You are truly appreciated.

To my mother, Elaine and my daughter Alissa. The two of you are like bookends mirroring different generations of strong and capable women. You have taught me so much and continue to challenge me to grow at every turn. I love you both and thank you for being with me on this journey.

To the main men in my life, Dani, Wilem and Bob (Dad). All three of you deserve a big thank you – for believing in me, supporting me and always asking for the best version of me to show up. I love you all and would not have nearly as much fun on this journey without you.

There are many other people I could thank, but not without risk of forgetting someone important. Thank you to the many wonderful women in my life – my nieces, friends, sisters, in-laws, colleagues, clients, pre-readers, healers and teachers – you all play an important role in my life and therefore the creation of this book. I would also like to thank the many males in my life that make me feel important and special despite my quirky nature.

Finally, a huge thank you to YOU– the reader. A book without a reader is just energy, bound together and waiting to be opened, appreciated and shared. Thank you for freeing my words and allowing them the opportunity to truly make a difference.

Suggested Resources

Debbie Pokornik, Empowering NRG, Helping People Reconnect to their inner wisdom and strength **debbiepokornik.com**

The following resources are a few of my favorite books or audios, along with some of the websites I like to 'hang-out' on. I've tried to divide them up into common categories, but there are many that overlap. Scan for the ones that jump out for you, or just search the internet for a topic of interest.

Connecting to the Feminine:

Brave Heart Women – Be. Create. Collaborate. **braveheartwomen.com**

Elegant Femme – For Women Who Are Ready to Be, Do & Enjoy It All **elegantfemme.com**

Feminine Power – The Keys to Feminine Power **femininepower.com**

Parenting Resources:

Debbie Pokornik, *Break Free of Parenting Pressures; Embrace Your Natural Guidance.* **empoweringnrg.com**

Mollie Wingate & Marti Woodward, *Slow Parenting Teens.*

Personal Development Resources:

Stephen Covey, *The 7 Habits of Highly Effective People* is perhaps his most famous book – I love them all. **FranklinCovey.ca**

Daniel Goleman, *Emotional Intelligence: Why It Can Matter More Than IQ*.

Sam Horn, *Tongue Fu! How to Deflect, Disarm and Defuse Any Verbal Conflict*.

Bruce H. Lipton, *The Wisdom of Your Cells: How Your Beliefs Control Your Biology*. Sounds True Audio Learning.

Stephanie Staples, *When Enlightening Strikes; Creating a Mindset for Uncommon Success*. **Yourlifeunlimited.ca**

Spiritual Development:

Amethyst Wyldfyre, Multi-dimensional Visionary Healer, Artist, Author, & Performer **AmethystWyldfyre.com**

For those feeling the feminine pull to share her message with large numbers of people, I highly recommend Amethyst and her colleague Mikael as a resource **TheEmpoweredMessenger.com**

Scott Blum, *Waiting for Autumn*. **DailyOm.com**

SoniaChoquette.com

Jerry & Esther Hicks, *The Astonishing Power of Emotions: Let Your Feelings Be Your Guide*. **Abraham-hicks.com**

Adam J Jackson, *The Ten Secrets of Abundant Happiness: Simple Lessons for Creating the Life You Want*.

Dan Millman, *The Way of the Peaceful Warrior*. **PeacefulWarrior.com**

Healing with the Masters is a cutting edge internet show where Jennifer McLean interviews different Masters for several weeks in a row. The interviews are free to listen to for a few days after each call with an option to purchase. **healingwiththemasters.com**

Understanding Relationships:

Alison Armstrong, PAX Programs – Your Source for Understanding Men & Women **Understandmen.com**

Gary Chapman, *The Five Love Languages; How to Express Heartfelt Commitment to Your Mate.*

John Gray, *Men are From Mars, Women are From Venus.*

Made in the USA
Charleston, SC
01 December 2012